CREDIT CARDS AND THE LAW

Revised and Updated by

by
Margaret C. Jasper

3rd Edition

Oceana's Legal Almanac Series:
Law for the Layperson

Oceana®
NEW YORK

OXFORD

UNIVERSITY PRESS

*Oxford University Press, Inc., publishes works that further Oxford University's
objective of excellence in research, scholarship, and education.*

Copyright © 2007 by Oxford University Press, Inc.
Published by Oxford University Press, Inc.
198 Madison Avenue, New York, New York 10016

Oxford is a registered trademark of Oxford University Press
Oceana is a registered trademark of Oxford University Press, Inc.

Library of Congress Cataloging-in-Publication Data

Jasper, Margaret C.
Credit cards and the law / by Margaret C. Jasper -- 3rd ed.
  p. cm. -- (Oceana's legal almanac series. Law for the
layperson)
  ISBN-13: 978-0-19-533896-6 ((clothbound) : alk. paper)   1. Credit Cards-
Law and legislation--United States--Popular works.   I. Title
  KF 1040.Z9J37 2007
  346'.7307'3--dc22
                                                          2007028083

Note to Readers:

This publication is designed to provide accurate and authoritative information in
regard to the subject matter covered. It is based upon sources believed to be accurate and reliable and is intended to be current as of the time it was written. It is sold
with the understanding that the publisher is not engaged in rendering legal,
accounting, or other professional services. If legal advice or other expert assistance
is required, the services of a competent professional person should be sought. Also,
to confirm that the information has not been affected or changed by recent develop-
ments, traditional legal research techniques should be used, including checking
primary sources where appropriate.

*(Based on the Declaration of Principles jointly adopted by a Committee of the
American Bar Association and a Committee of Publishers and Associations.)*

You may order this or any other Oxford University Press publication
by visiting the Oxford University Press web site at www.oup.com

To My Husband Chris

Your love and support

are my motivation and inspiration

To my sons, Michael, Nick and Chris

-and-

In memory of my son, Jimmy

Table of Contents

CHAPTER 2:
CREDIT CARD LEGISLATION

CHAPTER 3:
DEBIT CARDS, ATM CARDS AND GIFT CARDS

CHAPTER 4:
CREDIT CARD TERMS AND CONDITIONS

CHAPTER 5:
CREDIT CARD LOSS, THEFT AND UNAUTHORIZED USE

CHAPTER 6:
EQUAL CREDIT OPPORTUNITY

CHAPTER 7:
ESTABLISHING, MAINTAINING AND REHABILITATING CREDIT

ABOUT THE AUTHOR

MARGARET C. JASPER is an attorney engaged in the general practice of law in South Salem, New York, concentrating in the areas of personal injury and entertainment law. Ms. Jasper holds a Juris Doctor degree from Pace University School of Law, White Plains, New York, is a member of the New York and Connecticut bars, and is certified to practice before the United States District Courts for the Southern and Eastern Districts of New York, the United States Court of Appeals for the Second Circuit, and the United States Supreme Court.

Ms. Jasper has been appointed to the law guardian panel for the Family Court of the State of New York, is a member of a number of professional organizations and associations, and is a New York State licensed real estate broker operating as Jasper Real Estate, in South Salem, New York.

Margaret Jasper maintains a website at http://www.JasperLawOffice.com.

In 2004, Ms. Jasper successfully argued a case before the New York Court of Appeals, which gives mothers of babies who are stillborn due to medical negligence the right to bring a legal action and recover emotional distress damages. This successful appeal overturned a 26-year old New York case precedent, which previously prevented mothers of stillborn babies from suing their negligent medical providers.

Ms. Jasper is the author and general editor of the following legal almanacs:

AIDS Law
The Americans with Disabilities Act
Animal Rights Law
Auto Leasing
Bankruptcy Law for the Individual Debtor
Banks and their Customers
Becoming a Citizen

Buying and Selling Your Home
Commercial Law
Consumer Rights and the Law
Co-ops and Condominiums: Your Rights and Obligations As Owner
Copyright Law
Credit Cards and the Law
Custodial Rights
Dealing with Debt
Dictionary of Selected Legal Terms
Drunk Driving Law
DWI, DUI and the Law
Education Law
Elder Law
Employee Rights in the Workplace
Employment Discrimination Under Title VII
Environmental Law
Estate Planning
Everyday Legal Forms
Executors and Personal Representatives: Rights and Responsibilities
Harassment in the Workplace
Health Care and Your Rights
Health Care Directives
Hiring Household Help and Contractors: Your Rights and Obligations
 Under the Law
Home Mortgage Law Primer
Hospital Liability Law
How To Change Your Name
How To Form an LLC
How To Protect Your Challenged Child
How To Start Your Own Business
Identity Theft and How To Protect Yourself
Individual Bankruptcy and Restructuring
Injured on the Job: Employee Rights, Worker's Compensation and
 Disability Insurance Law
International Adoption
Juvenile Justice and Children's Law
Labor Law
Landlord-Tenant Law
Law for the Small Business Owner
The Law of Attachment and Garnishment
The Law of Buying and Selling
The Law of Capital Punishment

The Law of Child Custody
The Law of Contracts
The Law of Debt Collection
The Law of Dispute Resolution
The Law of Immigration
The Law of Libel and Slander
The Law of Medical Malpractice
The Law of No-Fault Insurance
The Law of Obscenity and Pornography
The Law of Personal Injury
The Law of Premises Liability
The Law of Product Liability
The Law of Speech and the First Amendment
Lemon Laws
Living Together: Practical Legal Issues
Marriage and Divorce
Missing and Exploited Children: How to Protect Your Child
Motor Vehicle Law
Nursing Home Negligence
Patent Law
Pet Law
Prescription Drugs
Privacy and the Internet: Your Rights and Expectations Under the Law
Probate Law
Protecting Your Business: Disaster Preparation and the Law
Real Estate Law for the Homeowner and Broker
Religion and the Law
Retirement Planning
The Right to Die
Rights of Single Parents
Small Claims Court
Social Security Law
Special Education Law
Teenagers and Substance Abuse
Trademark Law
Trouble Next Door: What to do With Your Neighbor
Victim's Rights Law
Violence Against Women
Welfare: Your Rights and the Law
What if It Happened to You: Violent Crimes and Victims' Rights
What if the Product Doesn't Work: Warranties & Guarantees

Workers' Compensation Law
Your Child's Legal Rights: An Overview
Your Rights in a Class Action Suit
Your Rights as a Tenant
Your Rights Under the Family and Medical Leave Act
You've Been Fired: Your Rights and Remedies

INTRODUCTION

This Almanac presents a discussion of the law governing the use of credit cards, including the historical background and development of the various credit card systems, and the credit protection legislation which necessarily ensued.

The role of an individual's credit history in credit granting decisions is also examined in this Almanac, as well as the legal protections afforded the consumer for preserving their credit rating. The complex nature of credit card finance is also explored.

This Almanac also sets forth the individual's rights and remedies when faced with unauthorized use of their credit card and identity theft. The individual's privacy rights are also discussed, particularly when using credit cards for online purchases.

Finally, because consumer debt has reached an all time high, with credit card debt being a major factor, a discussion of debt management and collection, and the laws which protect the debtor from harassment, threats and other illegal tactics is also set forth in this Almanac.

The Appendix provides tables and text of applicable statutes, and other pertinent information and data. The Glossary contains definitions of many of the terms used throughout the Almanac.

CHAPTER 1:
AN OVERVIEW OF
THE CREDIT CARD SYSTEM

WHAT IS A CREDIT CARD?

A credit card is basically defined as a small card, usually made out of plastic, which contains an account number, as described below, and a means of identification, such as a signature or picture. The credit card authorizes the person named on it to charge goods or services to the account, for which the cardholder is billed periodically.

A credit card is different from a debit or ATM card because it does not deduct money electronically from the cardholder's checking or savings account. Rather, the credit card issuer "lends" money for a purchase to the cardholder, and allows the cardholder to pay the balance off in full, or in installments, in which case the cardholder pays the issuer interest on the credit card balance. In addition, if the credit card company sends the cardholder a check to use against his or her account, this is also a loan that must be paid back, including the cost of the item purchased, accrued interest, and in some cases, an annual fee.

Although the names are often used interchangeably, the credit card is not the same as a charge card, which requires the cardholder to pay the balance in full at the end of the billing period.

HISTORY OF THE CREDIT CARD

Throughout history, people have used various methods of trading for goods and services. As needs changed, so did the methods of trading. The bartering system was replaced by money, and checks have been largely substituted for the exchange of money. As technology has advanced, alternate means of trading have been sought, and the credit card has in large part taken its place as an efficient substitute.

Credit cards have been in existence in some form since the early twentieth century. Prior to 1920, large department stores began to issue "credit coins"—small pieces of metal that displayed the name of the merchant and a series of numbers identifying the customer's account. These coins were issued to good customers, rewarding them by allowing them to purchase merchandise on credit in the store. In particular, these retail coins—precursors to retail credit cards—were supposed to build a loyal customer base and establish good will among affluent shoppers.

The use of credit cards originated in the United States during the 1920s, when oil companies began to issue charge plates to their customers for the purchase of gasoline and oil at their service stations. These early charge plates were usually made out of metal. Hotels also began to issue credit cards to their customers.

The Great Depression slowed the growth of consumer credit, and the use of credit was fairly insignificant until post-World War II. In 1950, Diners Club introduced the first independent charge card plan. The Diners Club plan involved agreements between the club and its members, and between the club and the merchants. This innovation was the brainchild of Alfred Bloomingdale, Frank McNamara and Ralph Snyder. Their novel concept involved the understanding that credit was a commodity that they would sell.

The Diners Club card became the first "universal" card which could be used at a variety of establishments. Under this system, the club charges its cardholders a fee to obtain the card, and an annual fee to keep the card. The club bills cardholders on a monthly basis. The members agree to pay each monthly bill. The merchant agrees to honor the card and then forward his credit vouchers to the club for monthly payment. Member merchants pay a service charge, which is a percentage of total billings.

As a result, the members are able to receive services and goods from various types of establishments by carrying only one card, and are able to pay one bill for all of these transactions at the end of the month. Among the benefits to the retail merchant is that it does not have to bother with designing, developing and administering its own credit card plan. The merchant is also likely to increase its volume of business because cardholding members find it more convenient to deal with a member merchant than with a merchant who wouldn't honor the cards.

The success of the Diners Club plan was so impressive that competitors soon followed their lead, trying to share in this new found source of wealth. For example, the American Express Company entered the field in 1958 and Hilton Credit Corporation initiated the "Carte Blanche" plan the following year.

These two formidable competitors were no newcomers to credit. American Express had been in the business of travelers checks and Carte Blanche was operated by the Hilton Hotel Corporation. In fact, American Express proved to be the most successful of the three. By 1976, American Express had ten times as many cardholders as Carte Blanche, and more than seven times the number of Diners Club cardholders. Nevertheless, Carte Blanche was considered to be the more prestigious of the three cards to hold.

Citibank purchased Carte Blanche and phased the card out of service in the late 1980s, but revived it in 1981 when Citibank acquired Diners Club. A new card was introduced—the Diners Club Carte Blanche Card— which proved to be a more formidable competitor to the popular American Express Platinum card.

In 1951, the First National Bank of Long Island became the first bank to offer its customers a credit card plan. However, such bank-issued credit card plans were not very important until 1959, when the Bank of America, a California-based bank, first issued its BankAmericard on a statewide basis. In 1966, it initiated a national network—a much-needed convenience for the growth of the credit card industry—by licensing the card in other states. The BankAmericard was subsequently renamed "VISA" in 1976-77.

Following in the footsteps of Bank of America, other large banks, such as Chase Manhattan Bank, began to issue their own credit cards. Another group of banks formed a national card system called the Interbank Card Association. In 1966, the Midwest Bank Card System was started. Another major bank credit card that developed was MasterCard—formerly known as Master Charge.

Many banks that began credit card plans on a local or regional basis have chosen to affiliate with major national-bank plans as the range of included services expanded. The bank credit card system has now spread to all parts of the world, including Communist nations.

With the advent of the bank credit card, the range of goods and services available on credit grew rapidly. This enabled consumers to purchase food, clothing, shelter, entertainment and travel with their new credit cards. By the beginning of the 1970s, personal and corporate credit cards had become fixtures in the nation's economy. In 1980, 56 percent of American adults had at least one credit card. Now, that number has grown to more than 76 percent, accounting for about $675 billion in outstanding credit card balances. In 2000, Americans charged more than $1 trillion ($1,000,000,000) in credit card purchases.

THE CREDIT CARD NUMBER

A credit card number is a special type of number—known as an ISO 7812 number—that complies with a certain standard set forth by the International Organization for Standardization (ISO). The number found on a credit card is made up of four parts:

1. The Major Industry Identifier – The major industry identifier is the first single digit in the credit card number. It identifies the industry within which the card is to be used.

2. The Issuer Identification Number – The issuer identification number is the first six digits in the credit card number, and includes the major industry identifier. The issuer identification number identifies the credit card issuer.

3. The Account Number – The account number is made up of a maximum of 12 digits, beginning with the sixth digit and ending with the second to last digit of the credit card number.

4. The Check Digit – The last digit of the credit card number is the check digit, also referred to as a checksum. The check digit uses a mathematical calculation involving the preceding numbers to detect and correct any errors.

THE CREDIT CARD IDENTIFICATION NUMBER

When paying by credit card, many businesses and merchants will request your credit card identification number to help protect you against fraudulent charges. The location of the credit card identification number depends on the type of card, as follows:

Visa, MasterCard and Discover Cards

Visa, MasterCard, and Discover cards have a 3-digit Card Security Code (CSC) located on the back of the card. This is the non-embossed number printed on the signature panel on the back of the card immediately following the card number.

The American Express Card

American Express cards have a 4-digit Confidential Identifier Number (CID) located on the front of the card. This is the non-embossed number printed above the account number on the front face of the card.

THE MAGNETIC STRIPE

The magnetic stripe on the reverse side of your credit card is swiped through the merchant's credit card terminal to complete a purchase. After it is swiped, the terminal contacts the "acquirer"—the organization that receives the credit card authentication request. Information obtained from the magnetic stripe includes the credit card number, credit limit, and the expiration date, in order to provide the merchant with a payment guarantee.

If the credit card reader is unable to read your card, it is likely due to a dirty or scratched magnetic stripe, or a magnetic stripe that has been erased or demagnetized. This may occur if the magnetic stripe is exposed to another magnet.

THE THREE-PARTY CREDIT CARD PLAN

The parties to a three-party credit card plan are the card issuer, the merchants who honor the credit card, and the cardholders who use the card to purchase goods and services. The card issuer's success is dependent upon its ability to solicit both merchants and prospective cardholders to participate in the plan. The card issuer distributes credit cards upon application by a prospective cardholder.

Credit Line

At the time the customer's application for a credit card is approved, the customer is given a maximum credit line—i.e., the credit limit. The available credit decreases as the cardholder uses the credit card, and is restored when the cardholder makes a payment on the account. Thus, at any given time, the credit available to the cardholder is dependent upon the amount owed to the card issuer. This is known as a "revolving credit" feature.

Purchasing Goods and Services

The credit card holder is entitled to purchase goods and services from any merchant member of the particular credit card plan. In return for this privilege, the cardholder has to pay the card issuer for "all credit extended on the basis of this card" or for "all purchases made with the card" until the issuer receives written notice of the loss or theft of the card.

Bill Payment

At the close of each billing period, the card issuer consolidates all of the purchases made by the cardholder from merchant members during the period and sends the cardholder one all-inclusive statement. Under this plan, upon receipt of each monthly statement, the cardholder has the option of either: (1) paying the total amount of the bill within a specified period—i.e., the "due date"—or (2) paying a portion of the amount due—e.g., the "minimum payment" — according to a deferred payment schedule. Of course, the cardholder is free to pay more than the minimum payment and reduce the principal balance accordingly.

The remainder of the outstanding balance is paid in monthly installments, and is subject to a finance charge—i.e., interest computed monthly at a specific percentage of the previous month's balance less all appropriate credits. Thus, the less the cardholder pays towards the principal balance, the more interest they will be charged.

Rights and Duties of Merchants

The rights and duties of the merchant members of the plan are contained in a form contract drafted by the card issuer. In general, the merchant is obligated to "assign" or "endorse" to the issuer all "sales drafts," "charge slips," or "accounts" which represent sales made to cardholders. With certain exceptions, the card issuer's "purchase" of these sales drafts or accounts is "without recourse" to the merchant in the event of nonpayment by cardholders. That means that the card issuer cannot seek reimbursement from the merchant if the cardholder does not pay their bill.

There are, however, some exceptions to this rule. For example, the card issuer may be able to recover its losses from the merchant if: (1) the merchant has accepted for payment an expired credit card; (2) a card is honored which is listed on the card issuer's void list provided to the merchant; (3) the sales slip is illegible or not signed by the person who made the purchase; (4) there is non-delivery of the merchandise; (5) there is a breach of warranty or fraudulent acts on the part of the merchant; or (6) the merchant, without prior clearance from the issuer, allows the cardholder to make a purchase in excess of the single-purchase limit established by the card issuer.

In other words, in those situations where the conduct of the merchant is responsible for improper validation of the purchase, the card issuer may hold the merchant liable.

In addition to assuming the credit risk, the card issuer handles the billing procedures, makes all collections from cardholders, and investigates the credit rating of card applicants. The issuer's compensation for these services is obtained by discounting the sales drafts assigned to it by the merchant at a rate established by the contract.

Bank Credit Cards

Bank credit cards are "third party" credit plans under which the company that provides the financial service has no affiliation with the buyer or seller of the goods and services purchased with the credit card. Bank credit cards offer highly flexible credit terms. Customers who can qualify for a fairly large credit limit—i.e., those who have a good credit history and adequate income—can incur relatively large indebtedness on such an account.

Also, by choosing to pay less than the entire balance due, cardholders can stretch out repayments over an extended period of time. Bank credit cards can therefore be used to satisfy fairly large needs for immediate credit and, if desired, scale repayments to available income. Furthermore, bank credit cards are widely accepted for purchases of a large variety of goods and services, and can also be used to obtain cash at many financial institutions. Nevertheless, cash withdrawals on credit cards are usually more expensive than purchases. Many card issuers charge immediate interest on cash advances even if they do not do so on purchases. There may also be a transaction fee deducted from the credit card account for each cash withdrawal.

Although the term "bank" credit card is commonly used, it obscures the growing diversity of institutions and organizations offering such services. "Bank" cards now are issued by finance companies, savings and loan associations, and credit unions. Although there are hundreds of different credit cards on the market, each with a variety of terms and conditions, a large percentage of them actually operate through the two major international credit card businesses, VISA and MasterCard. Thus, it is the VISA and MasterCard logo that is generally imprinted on the bank credit card, and the logo also appears in the windows of merchant members who accept the cards.

Co-Branded Cards

Many organizations have made arrangements with commercial banks to issue bank credit cards to members in the name of the organization. These cards are commonly referred to as co-branded cards. This practice has also become fairly popular with toy companies, such as Toys R Us; universities; organizations, such as AAA; and even baseball teams. The logo of the organization is imprinted on the card. These cards may provide incentives for the cardholder to use the card, such as cash back bonuses and frequent flyer mileage. The sponsoring organization receives a portion of the revenues generated.

Gold or Premium Cards

A variant of the bank credit card offered by many institutions is the so-called "gold" or "premium" card. Card issuers generally offer gold cards to its customers who appear to be a better than average credit risk, and who are generally in a higher income bracket than the national average. A gold card has a higher credit limit than an ordinary credit card and usually permits the cardholder to withdraw more cash.

The gold card combines the features of the regular bank credit card and a package of additional services that may include accident and other types of insurance, lost credit card services, hotel and car rental discounts, and no-fee travelers checks. Although these services are generally advertised as "free," they are not really free in that the cardholder pays for them through higher annual fees.

Although fees charged cardholders for "gold card" services are usually greater than the range of fees on regular bank credit card accounts, they are generally less than the fees charged for travel and entertainment cards, such as Diner's Club or American Express.

Travel and Entertainment Charge Cards

The universal charge cards discussed above—frequently referred to as "travel and entertainment cards"—are also three-party cards. Major issuers of such cards include American Express and Diners Club Carte Blanche. Like the less "upscale" bank cards, travel and entertainment cards also have "gold card" counterparts. However, there seems to be no foreseeable limit to the future gradations of such "premium" cards. This is demonstrated by the introduction of the American Express Platinum Card and it's rival, the Diners Club Carte Blanche card.

The travel and entertainment card is oriented toward more affluent customers able to pay a larger annual membership fee for access to premium credit card services. Since higher income requirements must be met to qualify for these cards, an element of prestige may be attached to carrying such cards as well as some presumption that cardholder creditworthiness is less subject to question than with other credit cards. Therefore, these programs appeal to customers who travel and/or entertain frequently, and for whom an easily accepted credit card with a relatively high credit limit can be especially convenient.

A variety of ancillary services is typically offered as part of a travel and entertainment card package. Travel accident insurance; discounts on travelers checks, hotel accommodations, and car rental; and access to check cashing are some examples of these additional services which may be offered.

A feature of most travel and entertainment cards is the requirement that balances be repaid within 30 days after billing. Thus, although the average balance for such accounts may be large, credit remains outstanding for only a relatively short period of time, so that gross financing costs incurred by the card issuers are kept fairly low in relation to the volume of billings. Card issuers also derive revenues from merchant discount charges paid by retailers.

THE TWO-PARTY CREDIT CARD PLAN

Although the three-party credit card plan is widely used, the original two-party credit card arrangement remains popular. In the two-party credit card transaction, the cardholder uses the credit card to make purchases at the store that issued the card. The cardholder either: (1) pays for their credit purchases in one lump sum at the next regular billing date; or (2) pays their charges on a revolving line of credit basis. There may also be a combination of these payment plans.

Retail Store Credit Cards

Two-party credit cards issued by retail stores are the most widely used type of credit card. For example, in 1981, Sears issued more cards than MasterCard or Visa. The use of retail store cards has continued to expand despite increasing competition from third-party credit cards, most of which are accepted by many retailers.

The large retail stores were not receptive to third party credit cards at first. Sears, J.C. Penney and Montgomery Ward were some of the staunchest opponents. However, in 1979, J.C. Penney gave in and signed an agreement with VISA to honor their credit cards.

Retail store cards typically have less demanding credit qualification requirements in comparison with third-party credit cards. Of course, use of retail credit cards is limited to the variety of merchandise carried by the issuing merchant. Retail revolving credit plans usually provide customers the option of repaying over an extended period of time.

AFFINITY CARDS

An affinity card operates like an ordinary credit card. It is not tied to a particular store but rather to a particular non-profit cause or benefit. The cardholder's charity receives a charitable contribution every time the cardholder uses the card for a purchase, cash advance or balance transfer. An affinity card bears the logo of the issuer and the charity. Generally, affinity cards have a higher than average interest rate and do not provide the user with any extra incentives or benefits in return for using the card. However, if the cardholder pays the bill in full each billing period, the interest rate is not an issue.

SECURED CREDIT CARDS

A secured credit card is one that is issued to the cardholder after he or she deposits a certain amount of money— from a few hundred to several thousand dollars—into a special savings account owned by the cardholder. A bank will generally pay interest on the deposit. The credit line is a percentage of the deposit, typically 50 to 100 percent. Thus, the line of credit is "secured" by the savings account.

There may also be substantial application and processing fees, therefore, it is advisable to find out the total amount of fees before applying for the card, and whether those fees are refundable. Typically, a secured card requires an annual fee and has a higher interest rate than an unsecured card.

The cardholder must make all of the required payments on the account just like a regular credit card, however, if the cardholder defaults on the payment, the issuer has the right to deduct that amount from the cardholder's savings account. The issuer reports the payment history to all of the credit reporting agencies. Thus, individuals who have been denied a credit card either because they have no credit history or a negative credit history can benefit from a secured credit card because it assists them in building good credit.

Nevertheless, the consumer must be aware of secured credit card scams that make deceptive advertising claims. The ads are designed to lead the consumer to believe they can get a card simply by calling the number listed in the ad. Sometimes the number is not toll-free. For example, the ad may advise the consumer to call a "900 number" to apply for the offer and the consumer will be billed just for making the call. The cost of the call can range from $2.00 to $50.00 or more.

The message may be no more than a recording instructing the consumer to leave their name and address to receive an application, or provide the consumer with a list of banks that offer secured credit cards. The deceptive ads do not provide the consumer with important information, such as the cost of the "900 number" call; the required security deposit and fees; eligibility requirements, such as age or income; and the high interest rate.

SMART CARDS

Smart cards use modern technology to provide even more security for cardholders. The smart card has an internal built-in microprocessor and uses cryptography—i.e., secret codes—to identify the cardholder instead of the authentication process currently being used. The smart card chip is capable of carrying out many types of transactions, including credit and debit card purchases.

Smart card technology requires the user to corroborate his or her identity to the card each time a transaction is made. The transaction itself is carried out in encrypted form to prevent anyone, including the cardholder and merchant, from accessing the information being transmitted through the terminal. It is expected that smart cards will eventually replace the plastic credit cards now in use.

INDIVIDUAL AND JOINT CREDIT CARD ACCOUNTS

There are two types of credit card accounts: (1) individual accounts; and (2) joint accounts. An individual account is opened in one person's name and is based only on that person's income and assets. A joint account is opened in two people's names, often a husband and wife, and is based on the income and assets of both or either person. Both people are responsible for the debt.

Authorized Users

If you open an individual account, you may authorize another person to use it. If you name your spouse as an authorized user, a creditor who reports the credit history to a credit bureau must report it in your spouse's name as well as in your name. A creditor also may report the credit history in the name of any other authorized user. However, the authorized user is not responsible for repayment of the debt.

THE PRESCREENED CREDIT CARD OFFER

Many credit card issuers solicit new customers by sending out offers for "pre-approved" cards. Potential new cardholders are located through a process known as prescreening. The companies obtain information from credit reporting agencies to find out if the customer meets the eligibility criteria. Although prescreening results in "inquiries" appearing in the consumer's credit profile, these inquiries have no negative effect on their credit report or credit score.

Nevertheless, consumers who do not want to receive prescreened credit offers can obtain information by contacting the opt out service set up by the credit reporting agencies, as follows:

Telephone: 1-888-OPTOUT (1-888-567-8688)

Online: www.optoutprescreen.com

The consumer will have the opportunity to opt out permanently or for a period of 5 years, but can opt back in at a future date using the same contact information. The consumer will have to provide certain personal information, such as their name, social security number and date of birth, however, the information is kept confidential. The opt out request is processed within 5 days but it takes up to 60 days for the prescreened offers to stop. In addition, opting out does not stop credit card solicitation letters that were not sent as a result of the prescreening process.

In addition to the opt out program discussed above, the federal government operates the national Do Not Call Registry as a means to reduce telemarketing calls. Consumers can register for this free service as follows:

Telephone: 1-888-382-1222

Online: www.donotcall.gov

The consumer must call from the number they want to register. It takes about 31 days for registration to become effective, and the registered telephone number will stay on the registry for 5 years until you take the number off or it is disconnected. The number can be re-registered after the 5-year period expires.

Federal law prohibits credit card issuers from sending a consumer a card they did not request. However, an issuer can send the cardholder a renewal or substitute card without a request.

CREDIT AND DEBIT CARD BLOCKING

When you rent a car or check into a hotel using a credit or debit card, the clerk estimates your final bill and contacts your credit issuer to have this amount approved on the card. This approved amount is reduced from your available credit, in the case of a credit card, or your bank account balance, in the case of a debit card. The amount held generally exceeds your total bill. This practice is called "blocking" or "holding." Its purpose is to make sure the merchant gets paid after services are rendered.

For example, if you rent a car for $50 per day for a total of three days, the rental company will hold $150 plus an additional amount in case you incur additional charges, such as gasoline, excessive mileage, etc.

After you return the car or check out of the hotel, if you pay your final bill with the same credit or debit card, the final amount will replace the blocked amount within 1 or 2 days. However, if you decide to pay cash or check, or use a different credit card, the block on the original credit or debit card may not be removed for up to 15 days because the creditor does not know that you paid the bill using another method of payment. Blocking may also be used in other situations, such as restaurants when you have a large party and the restaurant asks for you to provide your credit card in advance.

Ordinarily, blocking is not a problem if you have sufficient funds in your bank account, or you are not close to your credit limit. However, if you are low on available funds, blocking could lead to bounced checks and declined purchases while the block remains on your account.

To avoid blocking, when you are asked for your credit card in advance, ask the following questions:

1. Is the business going to block your card?
2. How much will be blocked?
3. How is the amount determined?
4. How long will the block remain in place?

If the business will be blocking, it is preferable to pay with the same card that was used for the blocking. Ask the clerk when the block will be removed. If you pay with a different card, by cash, or by check, remind the clerk you're using a different form of payment and ask them to remove the prior block promptly.

In addition, you should ask your creditor if they permit blocking, the type of merchants they allow to block, and how long the funds are blocked. If you generally use a debit card, you should consider applying for an overdraft line of credit to avoid any overdrafts or bounced checks caused by blocking.

CHAPTER 2:
CREDIT CARD LEGISLATION

THE CONSUMER CREDIT PROTECTION ACT

The Consumer Credit Protection Act was enacted by Congress in 1968 to afford protection to the individual consumer in obtaining credit and managing debt. The Act consists of six subchapters that deal with various consumer credit issues, including:

Subchapter I: The Truth in Lending Act

Subchapter II: Garnishment Restrictions

Subchapter III: The Fair Credit Reporting Act

Subchapter IV: The Equal Credit Opportunity Act

Subchapter V: The Fair Debt Collection Practices Act

Subchapter VI: The Electronic Funds Transfer Act

Subchapter I: The Truth in Lending Act

Subchapter I of the Consumer Credit Protection Act deals with disclosure of the cost of consumer credit, and is known as the Truth in Lending Act (TILA). The purpose of the TILA is ". . .to assure a meaningful disclosure of credit terms so that the consumer will be able to compare more readily the various credit terms available. . ." The TILA preempts any state laws that are inconsistent with its disclosure provisions. Regulation "Z" refers to the Federal Reserve Board regulations that implement the TILA provisions.

The Truth In Lending Act is discussed more fully in Chapters 4 and 5 of this Almanac.

Subchapter II: Garnishment Restrictions

Restrictions on garnishment were enacted as Subchapter II of the Consumer Credit Protection Act to protect the consumer from having an excessive number of garnishments placed on his or her income as a result of indebtedness.

Garnishment is discussed more fully in Chapter 8 of this Almanac.

Subchapter III: The Fair Credit Reporting Act

When a consumer applies for credit, such as a credit card, he or she generally fills out an application form which sets forth information concerning the consumer's creditworthiness. In considering the application, the creditor generally requests a report from a credit reporting agency to: (1) verify the information, (2) obtain additional information concerning the consumer's ability to take on additional debt, and (3) obtain the consumer's credit payment history, e.g. whether the consumer pays his or her bills on time.

All major credit granters routinely supply credit reporting agencies information concerning the payment history of its customers. The credit reporting agency also searches public records to determine whether the consumer has any judgments or liens filed which would affect their creditworthiness.

Credit reporting agencies are obligated to make sure the information contained in the consumer's file is current. The rationale for this requirement is to give the consumer a chance to rehabilitate a negative credit history. Maintaining information in this manner is helpful to both creditor and consumer provided it is accurate, and maintained in a manner so as to protect the applicant's privacy rights.

For example, the consumer must authorize the creditor to obtain his or her credit report. Unauthorized release of credit information may result in an action for invasion of the consumer's right to privacy. In addition, inaccurate information, such as negligently reporting the consumer as a late payer, may result in a defamation action.

Nevertheless, both of these remedies have their shortcomings when applied to consumer actions. In response to the inadequacy of these remedies, Congress enacted the Fair Credit Reporting Act (the "FCRA") in 1970 as Subchapter III of its Consumer Credit Protection Act. The FCRA preempts any state statutes that are inconsistent with its provisions.

The Fair Credit Reporting Act is discussed more fully in Chapter 7 of this Almanac.

Subchapter IV: The Equal Credit Opportunity Act

The Equal Credit Opportunity Act (the "ECOA") was enacted as Subchapter IV of the Consumer Credit Protection Act to prevent discrimination in the granting of credit based on certain criteria, including: (1) race; (2) national origin; (3) sex; and (4) marital status.

The Equal Credit Opportunity Act is discussed more fully in Chapter 6 of this Almanac.

Subchapter V: The Fair Debt Collection Practices Act

The Fair Debt Collection Practices Act (the "FDCPA") was enacted as Subchapter V of the Consumer Credit Protection Act in 1988 to supplement the statutory and common law tort remedies available to the debtor to restrain unfair debt collection procedures. The FDCPA contains detailed provisions regulating the manner in which debt collection is undertaken.

The Fair Debt Collection Practices Act is discussed more fully in Chapter 8 of this Almanac.

Subchapter VI: The Electronic Funds Transfer Act

The Electronic Funds Transfer Act (the "EFTA") was enacted as Subchapter VI of the Consumer Credit Protection Act for the purpose of providing a basic framework establishing the rights, liabilities, and responsibilities of participants in electronic fund transfer systems.

The Electronic Funds Transfer Act is discussed more fully in Chapter 3 of this Almanac.

THE FAIR CREDIT BILLING ACT

Billing Errors

The Fair Credit Billing Act (FCBA) establishes procedures for correcting billing errors. The law applies to "open end" credit accounts such as credit cards and revolving charge accounts. Under the law, card issuers must follow the rules for promptly correcting any billing errors, including:

1. Unauthorized charges;

2. Incorrect charges;

3. Math errors;

4. Failure to post payments and credits;

5. Failure to provide bills; and

6. Charges for which the cardholder has requested an explanation or written proof of purchase or clarification.

Most creditors do not provide copies of sales receipts with the monthly statement. The statement merely lists the merchant name, and the date and amount of the purchase. Therefore, the cardholder is advised to keep all of their sales receipts in order to check them against the statement to determine whether there has been a billing error.

If the cardholder suspects that there is a billing error, he or she must notify the card issuer, in writing, at the address specified for billing errors. This address usually appears on the billing statement. This notification must be made within 60 days after the first bill containing the error was mailed to the customer. Therefore, it is important for cardholders to review their credit card billing statements as soon as possible after receipt.

The billing error notification letter should include the name of the cardholder, the account number, the suspected error, the amount in dispute, and the reason why the cardholder believes the charge is in error. Include copies—not originals—of any documentation that supports the dispute, such as sales receipts. The letter should be sent by certified mail, return receipt requested, so there is proof of mailing. A copy of the letter and proof of mailing should be kept in a safe place until the dispute is resolved.

A sample notification of billing error is set forth at Appendix 1, (Notification Letter to Credit Card Issuer – Billing Error).

The law requires the card issuer to acknowledge the cardholder's letter within 30 days unless the card issuer corrects the billing error in less time. The card issuer is also required to investigate the error and either correct it or provide an explanation as to why they believe no error has been made. The card issuer has up to two billing periods, but no more than 90 days to respond.

A creditor who violates the rules for the correction of billing errors automatically loses the amount owed on the item in question and any finance charges on it, up to a combined total of $50 even if the bill was correct. The cardholder may also sue for actual damages plus twice the amount of any finance charges. The amount sought as damages must be a minimum of $100 up to a maximum of $1,000. The cardholder is also entitled to court costs and attorney's fees if the lawsuit is successful. A class action lawsuit—one filed on behalf of a group of people with similar claims—is also permitted under the law.

During the investigation period, the cardholder is entitled to withhold payment on the disputed amount while the error is being investigated. The card issuer cannot demand that the cardholder pay the disputed amount or any related finance charges or fees while the investigation is ongoing. In addition, the card issuer cannot report the account as delinquent.

The card issuer is required to correct the error promptly without damaging the cardholder's credit record. Until the card issuer responds to the problem, the law forbids it from taking any collection action of the disputed amount.

The cardholder must, however, still pay any part of the bill that is not in dispute, including finance and other charges. However, in order to take advantage of this protection, the cardholder must comply with the 60-day notification period discussed above.

If it is subsequently determined that there was no billing error, the card issuer is entitled to reinstate the charge, including any finance charges that accumulated and any minimum payments missed while the charge was being investigated. If the cardholder fails to pay the disputed amount at that point, the card issuer may then take legal action to collect the amount due and may report the overdue payment to a credit bureau.

If the cardholder continues to dispute the charge, the card issuer must report to the credit bureau that the cardholder has challenged the bill, and give the cardholder written notice of the name and address of each person who has received information about the dispute. If and when the dispute is resolved, the outcome must again be reported to each person who has received information about the account.

Defective Merchandise

In addition to regulating billing errors, the Fair Credit Billing Act also assists cardholders who have a dispute with a merchant concerning merchandise or services that were charged to their credit card. If the cardholder has not already paid off the balance, the law allows the cardholder to withhold payment that is still due for the disputed transaction, provided the cardholder has made a genuine attempt to solve the problem with the merchant. The cardholder can withhold payment up to the amount of credit outstanding for the purchase, plus any finance or related charges.

If the card used to make the purchase was a bank credit card, or a travel and entertainment card, or another card not issued by the merchant, the above protections still apply, however, the cardholder can withhold payment only if the purchase exceeded fifty dollars and occurred in the cardholder's home state or within 100 miles of their billing address.

Selected provisions of the Fair Credit Billing Act are set forth at Appendix 2, (The Fair Credit Billing Act – Selected Provisions).

RESOLVING YOUR CREDIT COMPLAINT

If you are having a credit problem covered by Federal law, you should first try to solve the problem directly with card issuer or other financial institution with whom you conduct business. If you are unable to resolve your problem at this level, you may file a written complaint with the Federal agency responsible for enforcing consumer credit protection laws, as set forth below.

Banks and Financial Institutions

If you have a complaint about a bank or other financial institution, you may file a written complaint with the Federal Reserve System. The Federal Reserve System investigates consumer complaints received against state-chartered banks that are members of the Federal Reserve System. Complaints about state-chartered banks are investigated by one of the 12 Federal Reserve Banks around the country. Complaints about other financial institutions are referred to the appropriate federal regulatory agency.

You should submit your written complaint to Federal Reserve in care of the following address:

Division of Consumer and Community Affairs,

Board of Governors of the Federal Reserve System,

Washington, D.C. 20551

In your written complaint, you should include the complete name and address of the bank, a brief description of your complaint, and copies—not originals—of any documentation that will support your complaint. The Federal Reserve will generally respond to your written complaint within 15 business days, and advise you whether the Federal Reserve will investigate your complaint or whether your complaint will be forwarded to another federal agency.

If the Federal Reserve handles the investigation, it will analyze the bank's response to your complaint to ensure that your concerns have been addressed, and will send you a follow-up letter discussing their findings. If the investigation reveals that a Federal Reserve regulation has been violated, you will be advised of the violation and the corrective action the bank has been directed to take.

Although the Federal Reserve investigates all complaints about the banks it regulates, it does not have the authority to resolve all types of problems, such as contractual or factual disputes of disagreements about bank policies or procedures. In many instances, however, if you file a complaint, a bank may voluntarily work with you to resolve your situation. If the matter is not resolved, you will be advised whether you should consider legal counsel to handle your complaint.

National Banks

File a complaint with the Office of the Comptroller of the Currency, Compliance Management, Mail Stop 7-5, Washington, D.C. 20219.

Federal Credit Unions

File a complaint with the National Credit Union Administration, 1776 G St., N.W., Washington, D.C. 20456.

Non-Member Federally Insured Banks

File a complaint with the Office of Consumer Programs, Federal Deposit Insurance Corporation, 550 Seventeenth St., N.W., Washington, D.C. 20429.

Federally Insured Savings and Loans, and Federally Chartered State Banks

File a complaint with the Consumer Affairs Program, Office of Thrift Supervision, 1700 G St., N.W., Washington, D.C. 20552.

CHAPTER 3:
DEBIT CARDS, ATM CARDS AND GIFT CARDS

WHAT ARE DEBIT AND ATM CARDS?

A debit or ATM card is linked to the cardholder's bank account. Although these cards are used in much the same way as an ordinary credit card, the cost of anything purchased, or money withdrawn from a bank automatic teller machine (ATM), will be deducted from the cardholder's bank account immediately. Thus, these cards effectively replace cash and checks, and reduce a bank's processing costs.

The ATM card is used at establishments that accept the ATM card as payment for goods and services, and at bank ATMs that accept the ATM card to withdraw money from the cardholder's bank account. When using an ATM card, the cardholder is generally required to enter their personal identification number (PIN) to complete the purchase.

The debit card, unlike an ordinary ATM card, usually carries the logos of one of the two major credit card companies—VISA or MasterCard, e.g., a "debit Visa" or a "debit MasterCard." The debit card can be used to make purchases anywhere the logos on these cards are accepted. When using the debit card for purchases, the cardholder is not required to enter their PIN number to complete the purchase. Debit cards are a convenient way for those persons who do not qualify for a credit card to make purchases without using checks or having to carry a large amount of cash.

Most issuers do not charge any fees for making purchases with a debit or ATM card. The purchases and ATM withdrawals are listed on the customer's monthly statement so they can track their spending and make sure there are no fraudulent transactions on the account. This is particularly important because, unlike a credit card where the bank suffers the loss incurred by fraudulent activity, when someone uses a debit card, the funds are immediately withdrawn from the cardholder's account. This could cause bounced checks, overdraft charges, etc., which may be very difficult to sort out and correct.

THE ELECTRONIC FUNDS TRANSFER ACT

The Electronic Fund Transfer Act (EFTA) provides consumers protection for all transactions using a debit card, ATM card, or other electronic means to debit or credit a consumer's bank account. The EFTA also limits a consumer's liability for unauthorized electronic fund transfers. Electronic funds transfer systems under the EFTA include:

1. Automated Teller Machines;

2. Pay-by-Phone services;

3. Direct Deposit and Automatic Payment services; and

4. Point of Sale Transfer systems, which permit a consumer to pay for goods and services by transferring funds simultaneously out of the consumer's account and into the seller's account at the time of purchase, e.g., using a debit or ATM card.

Covered Institutions

The EFTA defines a financial institution as: (1) a state or national bank; (2) a state or federal savings and loan association; (3) a mutual savings bank; (4) a state or federal credit union; or (5) any other entity that directly or indirectly holds an account belonging to the consumer. The definition is broad so as to include any entity that may offer electronic fund transfer services to a consumer.

Resolving Disputes

Under the EFTA, procedures have been established for resolving errors on bank account statements, including: (1) Electronic fund transfers that the consumer did not make; (2) Electronic fund transfers that are incorrectly identified or show the wrong amount or date; (3) Computation or similar errors; (4) The failure to properly reflect payments, credits, or electronic fund transfers; and (5) Electronic fund transfers for which the consumer requests an explanation or documentation, because of a possible error.

Under the EFTA, if there is a mistake or unauthorized withdrawal from your bank account through the use of a debit card, ATM card, or other electronic fund transfer, you must notify your financial institution of the problem or error not later than 60 days after the statement containing the problem or error was sent. Although most financial institutions have a toll-free number to report the problem, you should follow up in writing.

For retail purchases, your financial institution has up to 10 business days to investigate after receiving your notice of the error. The financial institution must tell you the results of its investigation within 3 business days of completing its investigation. The error must be corrected within 1 business day after determining the error has occurred. If the institution needs more time, it may take up to 90 days to complete the investigation, but only if it returns the money in dispute to the customer's account within 10 business days after receiving notice of the error.

Under the EFTA, there are three levels of liability that may be assessed against the consumer for unauthorized transfers.

1. If an unauthorized withdrawal is made from the consumer's account prior to the consumer being aware that his or her access card was lost or stolen, the consumer may be held liable for amounts withdrawn from the consumer's account prior to his or her notification to the financial institution, up to a maximum of Fifty ($50.00) Dollars.

2. If the consumer fails to notify the financial institution that his or her access card was lost or stolen within two business days of the consumer being aware of the loss, the consumer may be held liable for amounts withdrawn from the consumer's account prior to his or her notification to the financial institution, up to a maximum of Five Hundred ($500.00) Dollars.

3. If the consumer fails to report unauthorized transfers within 60 days of receiving a statement on which the unauthorized transfer appears, the consumer may have unlimited liability for amounts withdrawn from the consumer's account prior to his or her notification to the financial institution. That means the consumer could lose all the money in their account and the unused portion of their maximum line of credit established for overdrafts. The rationale for this apparently harsh rule is that the consumer would have to be unduly negligent for failing to notify the financial institution within that time period.

Some financial institutions may voluntarily cap a consumer's liability at Fifty ($50) Dollars for certain types of transactions, regardless of when they report the loss or theft. However, because this protection is offered voluntarily, the policies could change at any time. Thus, the consumer is advised to ask their financial institution about its liability limits.

The EFTA may not cover stored-value cards or transactions involving them, so the consumer may not be covered for loss or misuse of such a card. Thus, a consumer should inquire as to whether the issuer offers any protection in the case of a lost, stolen, misused, or malfunctioning card.

Remedies

If a financial institution does not follow the provisions of the EFTA, you may sue for actual damages—and in some cases, three times actual damages—plus punitive damages of not less than One Hundred ($100) Dollars nor more than One Thousand ($1,000) Dollars. You are also entitled to court costs and attorney's fees in a successful lawsuit. Class action suits are also permitted. If the institution fails to make an electronic fund transfer, or to stop payment of a preauthorized transfer when properly instructed by you to do so, you may sue for all damages that result from the failure.

LOST OR STOLEN DEBIT OR ATM CARD

If the debit or ATM card is lost or stolen, the cardholder must immediately report the loss to the bank that issued the card in order to limit their liability for unauthorized use. There are certain laws that protect the debit or ATM cardholder from liability if the card is lost or stolen. Under the EFTA, if the cardholder reports the loss to the issuer 2 business days after they discover that the card is missing, their losses are limited to a maximum of Fifty ($50) Dollars for any unauthorized use.

If the cardholder waits more than two business days to report the loss or theft, they are potentially responsible for any additional amounts resulting from their failure to notify the card issuer—up to Five Hundred ($500) Dollars. If the cardholder does not report the loss or theft within 60 days after receiving a bank statement that includes an unauthorized transfer, the law doesn't require the bank to reimburse the customer for any losses due to unauthorized transfers made after that 60-day period. Thus, the cardholder may be responsible for unlimited loss on transactions that occurred after the 60-day period.

Nevertheless, depending on the circumstances, if it is clear that the cardholder is an innocent victim of fraud, and he or she promptly reports the loss or theft of the card, or an unauthorized transaction, many banks will voluntarily hold the customer to no liability. Your bank may ask the cardholder to sign an affidavit or other notice of the loss or theft.

For the above reasons, it is important to save all ATM and debit receipts until they are reconciled with the bank statement. If there are any errors, they must be promptly reported to the bank. To be fully protected under the EFTA, in addition to reporting the loss or theft of a card, the customer must notify their financial institution of any errors, orally or in writing, no later than 60 days after the bank sends the bank statement containing the error.

It is preferable, however, to notify the financial institution by certified letter, return receipt requested, in order to prove that the institution received notice in a timely fashion. A copy of the letter and receipt should be kept in a safe place until the issue is resolved to the consumer's satisfaction.

USING THE ATM MACHINE

The ATM has been around since the mid-1960s. The first ATMs were strictly for getting cash using a bank-issued ATM card. Depending on the bank, in addition to dispensing cash, today's ATMs can accept deposits and loan payments, transfers funds between accounts, provides account information, including copies of canceled checks, and much more. Some ATMs even dispense postage stamps. When traveling in a foreign country, there will likely be an ATM somewhere that will be able to dispense cash using a debit or ATM card.

ATM Transaction Fees and Surcharges

ATMs are convenient, yet they can also be costly. For example, if you withdraw money from an ATM machine that is not owned by the bank that issued the card, the cardholder may incur a surcharge ranging from $1 to $4 per transaction. Federal law requires that an ATM alert a non-customer about a surcharge before a transaction is completed so the person can cancel the transaction if they wish.

To avoid unnecessary fees, it is best to try and use the issuing bank's own ATM whenever possible. Be aware that some banks also charge their own customers for ATM transactions, which may result in two charges—one from the ATM's owner, and the second from the card-issuing institution. In order to avoid surcharges altogether, the cardholder should request cash back when using a debit or ATM card to make purchases at a retail establishment, such as a supermarket, if that option is available.

Retained Card

On occasion, an ATM will not return the card to the customer following the transaction. Sometimes this is due to a defect in the card. This may also happen if the bank suspects fraudulent activity, e.g., if the customer repeatedly enters the wrong PIN number. If this should occur, immediately contact the financial institution that issued the card. They will issue a replacement card.

Error in Amount Dispensed

Sometimes an ATM malfunctions and does not dispense the amount of cash requested. If the receipt states that the amount of cash requested was dispensed, instead of the actual amount dispensed, immediately contact your bank to report the problem. The bank will check the machine to see if it has more money than it should have, in which case the difference will be refunded.

Recording ATM Withdrawals

It is important to record all ATM withdrawals and purchases in the check register. Failure to enter the information and account for the withdrawals can cause unnecessary overdrafts due to bad recordkeeping. When using the ATM to check balances and transactions, do not rely on the balance reflected by the ATM machine. The ATM balance does not reflect deductions for checks written but not yet paid. The only way to know how much money is available is to accurately maintain one's checkbook.

Safety Considerations

ATM manufacturers and financial institutions try to make ATM use as safe as possible. They install sophisticated cameras, place ATMs in safe locations, provide adequate lighting, limit the maximum daily cash withdrawals, and employ other security measures. Nevertheless, thieves still target ATM users. In order to reduce the possibility of becoming a victim, the following safeguards should be followed:

1. Know where your ATM card is at all times, and do not keep your PIN number written down anywhere on or near the card. A thief who has both the ATM card and PIN number can quickly withdraw money from your account. If possible, memorize the PIN number, and do not share the number with anyone. Destroy old ATM cards, cutting through the account number and magnetic strip before throwing the card away.

2. Only visit ATMs that are in safe, well-lit areas, particularly at night. If anyone is loitering at or near the ATM, stay away. Look around for unusual looking devices on or near the ATM that may be used to record or intercept your PIN number.

3. Protect your ATM card when you use it to make purchases at retail establishments. For example, if you give an employee your card and you notice that he or she swipes it through two devices instead of one, that second device could be recording your account information for use in making a fraudulent card. Report any suspicious activity to the bank that issued the card.

4. Be careful when using private ATMs, such as those located in retail establishments. These ATMS are not owned by financial institutions but by non-banking companies and individuals. It is better to use an ATM at a FDIC-insured bank. If you must use a private ATM, only use ATMs at establishments you trust. Private ATMs have been known to be a source of fraudulent activity by dishonest owners who collect card numbers for use in making duplicate cards.

5. Withdraw the dispensed cash safely and immediately put the money in your wallet or pocket. Do not count the money at the machine. When using a bank's drive-up ATM, keep the engine running, the doors locked, and roll up the window immediately after making the transaction.

GIFT CARDS

The use of gift cards as presents has become very popular. Many businesses and retail establishments now offer gift cards. Specially designed gift cards are widely available for every occasion. Gift cards have become the gift-buying solution for those people who are hard to buy for, or who already "have everything." The recipient of the gift card can buy whatever they want subject only to the monetary limit of the gift card.

Before purchasing a gift card, you should consider any terms and conditions that may affect the recipient's use of the gift card. For example, some gift cards can only be used at the store where you purchased the card. Other cards can be used for any in-store or online purchase with any retailer. In addition, some cards have expiration dates, or fees, e.g., if the card is lost or stolen, or inactive for an extended period of time.

FTC Tips for Purchasing Gift Cards

The Federal Trade Commission (FTC) has published the following tips for purchasing gift cards:

1. Buy from sources you know and trust.

2. Avoid buying gift cards from online auction sites because the cards may be counterfeit or may have been fraudulently obtained.

3. Read the fine print before you buy. If you don't like the terms and conditions, buy elsewhere.

4. When you're buying a card, ask about expiration dates and fees. This information may appear on the card itself, on the accompanying sleeve or envelope, or on the issuer's website. If you don't see it,

ask. If the information is separate from the gift card, give it to the recipient with the card to help protect the value of the card.

5. Inspect the card before buying. Verify that none of the protective stickers have been removed. Also make certain that the codes on the back of the card have not been scratched off to reveal a PIN number. Report tampered cards to the store selling the cards.

6. Give the recipient the original receipt to verify the card's purchase in case it is lost or stolen.

7. Consider purchase fees.

8. Consider fees for the recipient.

9. Check on purchase exceptions. For example, can the recipient use a store-specific gift card at either the physical store or at the store's website?

FTC Tips for Using Gift Cards

The Federal Trade Commission (FTC) has published the following tips for using gift cards:

1. Read the terms and conditions when you get the card, and check for an expiration date or any fees.

2. If you didn't receive the card's terms and conditions, the original purchase receipt, or the card's ID number, ask for them from the person who gave you the card, and then keep them in a safe place.

3. Treat your gift card like cash. If your card is lost or stolen, report it to the issuer immediately. You may be out the entire amount on the card. Some issuers don't replace the cards, but others do if you pay a fee. If an issuer charges for a replacement card, you'll most likely need to document the purchase and provide the ID number on the card. Most issuers have toll-free numbers to report lost or stolen cards.

4. If your card expires before you've had a chance to use it or exhaust its value, contact the issuer. They may extend the date, although they may charge a fee to do it. Some merchants have stopped charging inactivity fees or imposing expiration dates, so it pays to check with the issuer to make sure you've got the most up-to-date information.

Resolving Gift Card Problems

If you have a problem with a gift card, the first step is to contact the store or financial institution that issued the card. If you can't resolve the problem at that level, you may want to file a complaint with the appropriate authorities:

Gift Cards Issued by Retailers

Contact the Federal Trade Commission as follows:

Telephone: 1-877-FTC-HELP

Online: www.ftc.gov

Contact your state Attorney General's office as follows:

Online List of State Offices: www.naag.org

Gift Cards Issued by National Banks

The Office of the Comptroller of Currency (OCC) charters, regulates, and supervises national banks, some of which issue gift cards. Contact the OCC as follows:

Telephone: 1-800-613-6743

Email: customer.assistance@occ.treas.gov

CHAPTER 4:
CREDIT CARD TERMS AND CONDITIONS

IN GENERAL

Before selecting a credit card, the customer should investigate the terms and conditions which affect the overall cost of the credit. Under the Fair Credit and Charge Card Disclosure Act, the customer can compare terms and fees before they accept a credit card.

Every six months, the Federal Reserve System collects and publishes a report on the terms of credit card plans offered by financial institutions. This report includes information supplied by the largest card issuers in the country, as well as any other financial institutions that indicate to the Federal Reserve System that they would like to participate in the report and submit information about their credit card plans.

Although the credit terms listed in the Federal Reserve report are as of the date indicated and subject to change, the report gives the customer some starting point in researching the credit card with the best rates, terms and conditions.

THE TRUTH IN LENDING ACT

The Truth in Lending Act (TILA) deals with disclosure of the cost of consumer credit. The purpose of the TILA is ". . . to assure a meaningful disclosure of credit terms so that the consumer will be able to compare more readily the various credit terms available. . .". The TILA preempts any state laws that are inconsistent with its disclosure provisions. Regulation "Z" refers to the Federal Reserve Board regulations that implement the TILA provisions.

Under the TILA, a consumer has the right to obtain complete and accurate information concerning a particular transaction before making a final decision. Sellers and creditors are obligated under state and federal laws to provide the consumer with this information.

The TILA pertains to "creditors," who are defined as: (1) persons who regularly extend...consumer credit which is payable by agreement in more than four installments, or for which the payment of a finance charge is or may be required; and (2) persons to whom the debt arising from the consumer credit transaction is initially payable on the face of the indebtedness, or by agreement.

DISCLOSURE REQUIREMENTS

Under the federal Truth in Lending Act, every solicitation for a credit card must contain a brief disclosure statement setting forth the credit terms and conditions. More extensive disclosures are required with the application and following approval of the card. Disclosure must be made in writing and in a clear and conspicuous manner. Disclosures must be made in a timely manner so as to give the consumer a chance to consider them fully before entering into the transaction. In addition, specific disclosures concerning the finance charges and other fees must appear on the monthly billing statement. Some of the terms and conditions the customer should inquire about are set forth below.

YOUR CREDIT CARD PAYMENT

Your credit card payment depends on your account balance, the interest rate and the way your finance charge is calculated—the balance computation method—as discussed below.

The Interest Rate

Basically, the higher the interest rate, the more you will have to pay in finance charges over the time it takes you to pay off the account balance.

Periodic Interest Rate

The periodic interest rate is the interest rate you pay for a period of time less than one year. The card issuer is obligated to disclose the "periodic rate"—i.e, the rate the card issuer applies to the cardholder's outstanding account balance to figure the finance charge for each billing period.

Annual Percentage Rate

The annual percentage rate (APR) is a measure of the cost of credit expressed as a yearly rate. The APR was introduced as part of the Consumer Credit Act of 1974. The APR is required to be disclosed to the customer when he or she applies for a credit card, and again when the account is opened. It also appears on each monthly statement. Generally, the customer benefits from a low APR; however, the customer must make sure that the APR does not go up following the initial rate period.

Variable Rate Indexes

Some credit card plans allow the card issuer to change the APR on an account when interest rates or other economic indicators—known as "indexes"—change. Because the rate change is linked to the performance of the index, which may rise or fall, these plans are commonly called "variable rate" plans. Rate changes raise or lower the amount of the finance charge the cardholder pays on their account.

Some of the more common indexes used by credit card issuers who issue variable rate cards are the prime rate, the one-month, three-month, or six-month Treasury Bill rate, the federal funds, or Federal Reserve discount rate. Most of these indexes can be found in the money or business section of major newspapers.

Once the interest rate corresponding to the index has been identified, the issuer then adds a number of percentage points, known as the "margin," to this index rate to calculate the rate charged. In some cases, the issuer might elect to use another formula to determine the rate to be charged to the consumer. The issuers multiply the index or index plus the margin by another number, "the multiple," to calculate the rate charged.

If a credit card has a variable rate feature, the card issuer is obligated to tell the customer that the rate may vary, and how the rate is determined, including the index used and the margin that will be added to the index to determine the new rate. The customer should also be advised how much and how often the rate may change.

Usury Laws

Many state laws provide that an individual cannot lend money at an interest rate that exceeds the state's statutory maximum—i.e., "the usury limit." "Usury" is generally defined as charging a price for credit that exceeds the usury limits set by law. Some states have no established usury limit. In addition, there are presently no federal usury limits. The federal government relies on the Truth in Lending Act, which guarantees that lenders disclose their rates, fees and terms.

You may notice that your state has a reasonable usury limit, such as twelve percent (12%), but your credit card carries an interest rate of twenty-five percent (25%). The reason for this huge gap in permissible interest is that the interest rate assessed on your credit card is the rate established by the state in which the bank's credit card operations are situated. As long as the credit card issuer abides by the law of the state in which their credit card operations are located, the interest rates and fees they assess are legal, even if the consumer lives in a state that has a much lower usury limit. Most credit card issuers move their operations to the states that have these lender-friendly interest caps and few restrictions.

Therefore, it is advisable to take notice of the state in which the credit card operations for your credit cards are located, as this may indicate how high your credit card interest rates may rise, particularly if you make a late payment or otherwise default on your credit card agreement. Generally, credit card issuers include a provision in the credit agreement that allows them to raise your interest rate to their highest "default" rate if you fail to abide by any of the credit card terms, e.g. by exceeding your credit limit or making a late payment.

Presently, there are 26 states that have no limit on what bank credit card issuers can charge for interest rates, and 27 states have no limit on what they can charge for annual fees. California, Delaware, South Dakota and Tennessee have no set maximums on what they can charge for delinquency fees, cash advance fees, overlimit fees, transaction fees, ATM fees, etc., and do not provide any type of grace period. It is no coincidence that many credit cards are issued under the laws of those four states.

A table of state usury laws is set forth at Appendix 3 of this Almanac.

The Finance Charge

The most important disclosure requirement of the TILA relates to finance charges. The finance charge is defined as "the sum of all charges payable directly or indirectly by the person to whom the credit is extended and imposed directly or indirectly by the creditor as an incident to the extension of credit." This would include such items as: (1) interest; (2) service charges; (3) loan fees; (4) insurance premiums; and (5) other similar fees.

Balance Computation Methods

If a credit card plan has no free period, or if you expect to pay for purchases in installments, it is important to know how the card issuer will calculate the finance charge. This charge varies depending upon the method the card issuer uses to figure the balance. The method used can make a difference in how much finance charge the customer will pay. This is so even when the APR is identical to that charged by another card issuer, and the pattern of purchases and payments is the same. The balance computation method must appear on the credit card application as well as on each monthly statement.

Average Daily Balance Method

The average daily balance method gives the cardholder credit for their payment from the day the card issuer receives it. To compute the balance due, the card issuer totals the beginning balance for each day in the billing period and deducts any payments credited to the account that day. New purchases may or may not be added to the balance, depending on the plan, but cash advances are typically added. The resulting daily balances are added up for the billing cycle and the total is then divided by the number of days in the billing period to arrive at the "average daily balance." This number is then multiplied by the monthly interest rate to determine the finance charge. This is the most common method used by credit card issuers.

Adjusted Balance Method

The adjusted balance method is computed by subtracting the payments made and any credits received during the current billing period from the balance the cardholder owed at the end of the previous billing period. This amount is then multiplied by the monthly interest rate to determine the finance charges. New purchases made during the billing period are not included. Under the adjusted balance method, the cardholder has until the end of the billing cycle to pay part of their balance and avoid the finance charges on that portion. Some creditors exclude prior, unpaid finance charges from the previous balance. The adjusted balance method is usually the most advantageous to cardholders.

Previous Balance Method

The previous balance method simply factors in the amount owed at the end of the previous billing period. The previous statement's balance is multiplied by the monthly interest rate to determine the finance charge. Payments, credits, or new purchases made during the current billing period are not taken into account. Some creditors also exclude unpaid finance charges in computing this balance. The previous balance method is usually the most advantageous to card issuer.

The Grace Period

The grace period—also known as the free period—refers to the amount of time given the cardholder to pay their bill in full without incurring a finance charge. Knowing whether a credit card plan gives you a grace period is especially important if the cardholder plans to pay their account in full each month.

If there is no grace period, the card issuer will impose a finance charge from the date the card is used, or from the date each transaction is posted to the account. If the credit card plan has a grace period, the card issuer must make sure the payment is posted by the due date.

As set forth below, a card with a grace period may afford the cardholder almost two months in interest-free credit.

Interest-Free Credit

In order to use your credit cards interest-free, you must first make sure that you have a credit card with a grace period—a card which does not start charging you interest from the date the transaction is made. If the credit card issuer charges interest from the statement date, and only imposes the interest if the account is not paid in full, the customer can obtain a substantial period of interest-free credit.

For example, if the earliest transaction occurs up to 1 month before the statement date, and the card issuer is given a grace period—e.g. 25 days—within which to make the payment, this could result in almost 2 months of interest-free credit. Thus, a customer who expects to pay their entire account balance each statement period would be wise to shop around for a credit card that charges no annual fee and has the longest "interest-free" period.

Transaction Fees and Other Charges

There may be a number of other costs which appear on the credit card statement. For example, some card issuers charge late payment fees, overlimit fees, and cash advance fees, as set forth below.

Overlimit Fees

Credit card issuers generally set a limit on the amount of credit that they are willing to provide the cardholder. This is known as the credit limit. Many banks charge the cardholder an "overlimit fee" if they exceed this limit. An overlimit fee can be substantial—e.g., anywhere from Twenty Five ($25) Dollars to Fifty ($50) Dollars.

It is often difficult to ascertain whether or not one has exceeded their credit limit during a billing period unless the cardholder keeps very careful track of their receipts, and factors in the applicable finance charge and fees which may be assessed. Further, because the credit card issuer generally authorizes purchases that exceed the credit limit as a courtesy to the cardholder, it is possible to exceed one's credit limit unknowingly and wind up having an overlimit charge appear on the next billing statement. Most credit card issuers will waive this fee one time as a courtesy for the cardholder.

To avoid this situation, if the cardholder believes they may be approaching their credit limit, they are advised to call and check their available credit prior to making a purchase, and keep in mind any applicable finance charges and fees. The cardholder may contact the credit card issuer and request that they deny any purchases that will put the account over the limit. The only other alternative is to shop around for a credit card that does not charge an overlimit fee.

Late Fees

Some credit cards with initial low rates will assess a high annual percentage rate (APR)—sometimes in excess of 25%—if the cardholder is late with their payments for a certain number of times in any specified time period. The delinquency rate will usually apply until the account balance is paid and the account is closed. If a credit card plan has a delinquency rate feature, this should be disclosed to the customer in the solicitation or credit card application. The consumer is advised to carefully read these disclosures.

Annual Fee

The annual fee refers to a membership fee charged by most credit card issuers each year. The annual fee for gold or premium cards is generally higher than the annual fee for an ordinary credit card.

THE MINIMUM PAYMENT

Unfortunately, credit comes at a very costly price. As set forth above, interest rates can go as high as 30% or more, with additional fees and penalties tacked on for late payments, exceeding the credit limit, annual fees, etc. The result is that the average consumer can never pay off the principal balance, especially if he or she sticks to the minimum payment requested, keeping them forever in debt.

The average American household now has approximately $7,300 of credit card debt, and the average credit card interest rate is 16.75%. At this rate, it could take 44 years to pay off this credit card debt, and cost the consumer over $16,000 in interest if he or she continues to pay the minimum payment due, which many consumers choose to do. Fortunately, 42% of credit card holders now pay off their balances in full each month, thus avoiding interest. Of course, credit card issuers are not happy when a credit card balance is paid off in full because it cuts into their profits.

Recognizing that paying the minimum payment requested on a credit card keeps the consumer indebted for many years, the Office of the Comptroller of Currency (OCC) instituted new rules regarding minimum credit card payments. The new rules went into full effect in 2005. Under the new rules, the minimum monthly payment amount for a credit card increased from 2% to 4% or more, depending on the bank that issued the credit card.

The minimum payment increase has been met with mixed reviews. Some consumers are unhappy that they have to increase their limited budget for credit card payments while others recognize that raising the minimum payment will help them pay down their debt much sooner.

INTRODUCTORY RATES

Many card issuers now quote low introductory rates of between 0 and 10% for the first year to attract new customers. However, the customer must find out what the interest rate will revert to once the introductory period ends, and whether the introductory rate covers the transfer of outstanding balances from other credit cards until they are paid.

The customer must also find out when the card issuer will start charging interest. If they start charging interest from the date the transaction is made rather than the statement date, the card may actually end up being more expensive because the customer is paying interest from the moment of purchase.

CREDIT CARD INSURANCE

Credit cardholders are often asked whether they would like to purchase optional credit insurance. Credit insurance protects the cardholder in certain situations:

1. Credit Disability Insurance – The minimum payment is paid on the cardholder's behalf if he or she becomes medically disabled. Payments are made over a pre-determined period of time. Any transactions made following the cardholder's disability claim are not covered. This insurance option is designed to protect the cardholder's credit rating during their period of disability.

2. Credit Life Insurance – The balance owed on the cardholder's credit card will be paid in full if the cardholder is deceased. The beneficiary of the insurance is the credit issuer.

3. Credit Property Insurance – Cancels the balance on items purchased with the credit card if the item is completely destroyed as specified in the insurance policy.

4. Unemployment Credit Insurance – The minimum payment is paid on the cardholder's behalf if he or she becomes unemployed due to an involuntary lay-off or company downsizing.

The cost of the credit insurance is a monthly premium computed as a percentage of the existing credit balance and deducted from the credit card's available balance.

REMEDIES

If a creditor violates the TILA, it is liable to the consumer for actual damages. For example, an understatement of the finance charge may result in actual damages to the consumer computed as the difference between the finance charge as stated, and the finance charge as actually assessed. Nevertheless, if actual damages are not present, violations of the TILA still result in liability as set forth in the statute. Further, a consumer who prevails is generally entitled to legal fees expended in enforcing the statute.

CHAPTER 5:
CREDIT CARD LOSS, THEFT AND UNAUTHORIZED USE

RISK OF LOSS

When an individual loses cash, it's gone and there is nobody to look to for reimbursement. Due to federal legislation in this area, the same does not hold true with the loss or theft of a credit card, and unauthorized charges made to the lost or stolen card. Nevertheless, virtually all credit card issuers attempt to shift the risk of unauthorized purchases to the cardholder until he or she gives the issuer written notice of the loss, theft or unauthorized use of the card.

RISK-SHIFTING UNDER THE THREE PARTY CREDIT CARD PLAN

The risk shifting process goes through three stages in the three-party credit card arrangement:

1. The cardholder is supposed to bear the risk of loss for all purchases made by an unauthorized user between the date of loss or theft of the card and the time that written notice is received by the appropriate office of the credit card issuer.

2. The issuer then bears the risk of loss between this date and the date that it gives written notice to all of its affiliated merchants, hotels, restaurants, etc.

3. The risk of loss then passes to the affiliated merchant or business if it should honor a credit card after the merchant or business has been notified that the card has been cancelled because it was lost or stolen.

RISK-SHIFTING UNDER THE TWO PARTY CREDIT CARD PLAN

The risk shifting process under the two-party credit card arrangement is more abbreviated. The risk of loss is on the cardholder until he or she gives written notice of the loss or theft of the card. Since the issuer and the honoring store are the same in the two party credit card arrangement, there is no risk shifting between the issuer and any third party merchants or businesses.

GOVERNING LAW – CIVIL LIABILITY

State Law

A number of states have enacted legislation to limit cardholder liability for unauthorized use. One approach allowed the issuer to enforce the notice clause only if: (1) the cardholder requested the card; or (2) the cardholder used an unsolicited card after receiving it. Another approach held the cardholder liable only if he did not take reasonable steps to discover the possibility of unauthorized use or did not give notice within a reasonable time after discovering the loss or theft.

Due to the confusing state judicial and statutory approaches to limiting cardholder liability for unauthorized use, Congress decided to enact legislation to ensure uniformity and to more fairly allocate the burden of loss between card issuers and cardholders.

The Truth in Lending Act

The federal Truth in Lending Act (TILA) was amended to virtually eliminate cardholder liability for the unauthorized use of credit cards. Under TILA, the cardholder is liable for its unauthorized use: (1) only if the card is an accepted card—i.e., not an unsolicited card; and (2) only to the extent of Fifty ($50) Dollars. Further, the unauthorized use of the credit card must occur before the cardholder has notified the card issuer that an unauthorized use has occurred or may occur as the result of loss or theft.

The card issuer must give adequate notice to the cardholder of the potential liability, and must provide the cardholder with a self-addressed stamped notice to be mailed by the cardholder in the event of loss or theft of the credit card. For the purposes of determining whether the card issuer has been properly notified, a cardholder notifies a card issuer by taking such steps as may be reasonably required in the ordinary course of business to provide the card issuer with the pertinent information whether or not the card issuer received this information.

This provision is not applicable in a situation where a cardholder voluntarily and knowingly allows another person to use his credit card and that other person subsequently misuses the card. Unauthorized use of a credit card occurs only where there is no actual, implied, or apparent authority for such use by the cardholder.

In any action by a card issuer to enforce liability for the unauthorized use of a credit card, the burden of proof is on the card issuer to show that the use was authorized, or that the conditions of liability for the unauthorized use have been met.

Unauthorized Use Defined

TILA defines "unauthorized use" as "use by a person other than the cardholder who does not have actual, implied or apparent authority for such use, and from which the cardholder receives no benefit." The statute does not define the meaning of "actual, implied or apparent authority." According to the Federal Reserve Board—the entity responsible for interpreting TILA and its regulations—whether actual, implied or apparent authority exists is to be determined under state or other applicable law.

Apparent Authority

While it is clear that unauthorized use of another's credit card by a finder or a thief is the intention and meaning of the statute, it is less clear whether unauthorized use includes use by another who initially was authorized, but whom the cardholder no longer authorizes to use the credit card. In this regard, one court stated:

> "We hold that in instances where a cardholder, who is under no compulsion by fraud, duress or otherwise, voluntarily permits the use of his (or her) credit card by another person, the cardholder has authorized the use of that card and is thereby responsible for any charges as a result of that use." Martin v. American Express, Inc., 361 So. 2d 597 (Ala. App. Ct. 1978).

On the other hand, the Federal Trade Commission, invoking the TILA provision, ordered a card issuer to limit the liability of certain cardholders for charges made by persons whom those cardholders had voluntarily permitted to use their credit cards.

Thus, there is considerable confusion and inconsistency for resolving cases dealing with the meaning of unauthorized use. The following cases highlight the prevailing unpredictability concerning unauthorized use.

Walker Bank & Trust Co. v. Jones

In Walker Bank & Trust Co. v. Jones, 672 P.2d 73 (Utah Sup. Ct. 1983), the bank tried to recover charges from their customer, Mrs. Jones, that were incurred by her estranged husband, Mr. Jones. Mrs. Jones claimed that violations of TILA absolved her of liability and rendered the bank liable for her husband's charges.

Mrs. Jones had established Visa and Master Charge accounts with the bank in 1977. At her request, the bank issued credit cards on those accounts to Mrs. Jones and Mr. Jones in each of their names. Although Mr. Jones received a credit card in his own name, he was not a "cardholder." According to TILA, a cardholder is "any person to whom a credit card is issued or any person who has agreed with the card issuer to pay obligations arising from the issuance of a credit card to another person." An interpretation of this section by the Federal Reserve Board clarified Mr. Jones' status: Where one spouse opens a "family account," only that spouse is considered a "cardholder" regardless of the names in which the cards are issued.

In November 1977, Mrs. Jones wrote the bank two letters indicating that she would no longer honor her estranged husband's charges on the two accounts. Pursuant to a clause in the cardholder agreement, the bank revoked the accounts and requested the return of all credit cards. Both Mrs. Jones and her husband retained their cards, however, and continued to make charges against the accounts. The cards were not returned until March 1978. By then, the balance on the accounts was $2685.70, which the bank sued to recover.

The only issue before the Utah Supreme Court was whether Mrs. Jones was entitled to TILA protection for her husband's use of the credit card. In a split 3-2 decision, the court affirmed the lower district court's summary judgment for the bank, and held that Mr. Jones' use of the credit card was not "unauthorized" within the meaning of TILA. The court further held that the protections of the law did not apply and Mrs. Jones was liable under the cardholder agreement.

Again, the pivotal question was what constitutes "unauthorized use." Both the majority and dissenting opinions noted TILA's definition of unauthorized use:

"Use by a person other than the cardholder who does not have actual, implied, or apparent authority and from which the cardholder receives no benefit."

While the majority and the dissent seem to agree that Mr. Jones was not a "cardholder" within the meaning of TILA, and that Mr. Jones had no actual or implied authority, the opinions split on whether he acted with apparent authority.

The majority held that apparent authority exists when "a person has created such an appearance of things that it causes a third party reasonably and prudently to believe that a second party has the power to act on behalf of the first person." Mrs. Jones created such an appearance when she requested that her husband receive a credit card bearing his own name and signature, leading third party merchants reasonably and prudently to conclude that Mr. Jones was authorized to use the card even if he was not.

Mrs. Jones' notification to the bank that further use of the credit card by Mr. Jones was unauthorized did not revoke his apparent authority. Therefore, the majority held that Mr. Jones acted with apparent authority and TILA did not apply to limit Mrs. Jones' liability.

The majority also focused on the terms of the cardholder agreement and found that because Mrs. Jones did not surrender all of the credit cards issued on her account immediately upon the bank's request, she was liable for all the charges incurred.

This case stands for the proposition that use of a credit card by an estranged spouse after cardholder notification that the use is no longer authorized is not "unauthorized use" within the meaning of TILA because such use is clothed with apparent authority.

Critics of the Walker decision have suggested that the courts should follow the principles of the law of agency and determine in these situations whether the cardholder acted reasonably in each case. In this case, it would have been reasonable to require the cardholder to notify the bank and return her own cards, and not impose the unreasonable burden of returning all of the credit cards issued on her account.

Martin v. American Express, Inc.

In Martin v. American Express, Inc., 361 So. 2d 597 (Ala. App. Ct. 1978), the cardholder authorized another person to use the card with the condition that the authorized user not exceed $500 in charges on the card. The cardholder also wrote to the card issuer requesting that amounts charged not exceed $1,000. Nevertheless, the court held that the cardholder was liable for any purchases made through the use of his card by anyone authorized to use it. Unauthorized use of a card occurs only where there is no actual, implied or apparent authority.

This case stands for the proposition that where a cardholder allows another person to use his or her credit card, and that person exceeds the authority given by charging more than he or she was authorized to charge, the cardholder remains responsible for those excessive purchases.

Cleveland Trust Co. v. Snyder

In Cleveland Trust Co. v. Snyder, 380 N.E.2d 354 (Ohio Ct. App. 1978) a husband requested and received a bank credit card. The husband subsequently requested a card for his wife without requiring her to complete or sign an application. The wife was issued a card under the husband's account as an authorized user. The husband received cash advances which were charged to his account but which he did not repay. The court held that the card issuer could not hold the wife liable for the husband's unpaid debts because she was merely a recipient of a related card, and not an original cardholder.

Unsolicited Credit Cards

A large number of states have enacted statutes which provide that a person who receives an unsolicited credit card which he does not accept—by use or authorization of use—is not responsible for any liability resulting from its loss or theft, and failure to return or destroy an unsolicited card does not constitute acceptance.

GOVERNING LAW - CRIMINAL LIABILITY

Depending on the jurisdiction and circumstances, criminal liability may be imposed for theft and unauthorized use of a credit card, as discussed below.

State Laws

Larceny

Under the general criminal statutes of most states, credit purchases made with a stolen credit card—or otherwise unlawfully obtained card—fall under the offense of larceny.

In addition, a person who obtains a credit card by misrepresentation, and then uses the card to purchase goods or services on credit, commits larceny the same as one who directly obtains property from the owner by false pretenses. It may be possible to prosecute someone who obtains a credit card by false pretenses even though he does not use it.

If a cardholder uses his or her credit card after the expiration date, the outcome is unpredictable. While many states have enacted statutes making it a criminal offense to use a credit card after it has expired or has been revoked, it is questionable whether in the absence of such a statute a cardholder could be successfully prosecuted under general larceny statutes. This is especially unlikely if there is no strong showing of criminal intent to defraud.

Although knowing use of an expired or revoked card is prohibited where notice of the revocation has been given to the person to whom the card is issued, in some states, the violation is restricted to knowing use with intent to defraud.

A few states provide that the presentation of an expired or revoked card is prima facie evidence of knowledge that the card is expired or revoked unless the purchaser, within ten days after receipt of notice that the card has expired or been revoked at the time of the purchase, makes payment in full of the amount due on such purchase. The notice of revocation or expiration in that case must also state the amount due on such purchase.

Forgery

Under most credit card plans, the cardholder is required to sign a receipt, invoice or other document for the merchandise or services received. If someone other than the legitimate cardholder signs the cardholder's name to such a document without the cardholder's authority, the crime of forgery has been committed.

In addition, the material alteration of a credit card such as by change of name, number of expiration date, and its subsequent use, would constitute a criminal offense in the area of forgery or larceny.

Model Penal Code

Section 224.6 of the Model Penal Code provides that it is an offense to use a credit card for the purpose of obtaining property or services with knowledge that the card is stolen, forged, revoked, cancelled, or for any other unauthorized reason. Some state codes have followed the Model Code by not requiring any criminal state of mind beyond knowledge that use of the card is unauthorized. On the other hand, a number of the newer codes as well as many older ones require an "intent to defraud."

Section 224.6 distinguishes between (1) the use of stolen, forged, revoked, or cancelled cards from (2) the use of cards outside the authorization of the card issuer. The section also sets forth an affirmative defense in the latter case upon proof that the cardholder had the ability to meet all of his or her obligations to the issuer arising out of use of the card.

The circumstances chiefly contemplated by this section were (1) use by the holder of an expired credit card; and (2) situations where the user exceeded credit limits established by the card issuer. The rationale for this view is that it is wrong to penalize good faith use of a card by someone to whom it had been issued merely because he or she has delayed or omitted some minor step required to maintain the right to continue using the credit card, or because he or she has failed to adequately keep track of a few charges previously incurred.

Grading Credit Card Offenses

The Model Penal Code grades credit card offenses as a felony of the third degree where the amount involved is over $500, and a misdemeanor if the amount involved is less than $500. The states have adopted a variety of approaches and standards in establishing misdemeanor and felony categories. A few states have followed the Model Penal Code approach, although the dividing point between felony and misdemeanor varies. A number of states agree in principle with using the amount involved as a means to distinguish between felony and misdemeanor, but define the amount involved not from a single transaction but from a series of transactions within a given time period.

Criminal Prosecution Under Federal Law

In addition to the possibilities of prosecution under state law, the misuse of a credit card under certain circumstances may give rise to prosecution under various federal criminal statutes, as discussed below.

The federal Mail Fraud Statute (18 USCS §1341) prohibits the use of the mail "for the purpose of executing" a scheme to defraud, This statute has been interpreted by the federal courts to be broad enough to cover the procurement of a credit card by misrepresentation in order to perpetrate a fraud, or to carry out a fraud through the use of a stolen or forged credit card, providing that the use of the mail was a significant step in the execution of the fraudulent scheme.

The federal Truth in Lending Act also imposes criminal liability for the wrongful use of credit cards. The statute broadly proscribes the fraudulent use of credit cards in interstate or foreign commerce, or transactions affecting such commerce, and includes counterfeit, fictitious, altered, forged, lost, stolen, or fraudulently obtained credit cards.

Criminal Elements

Intent to Defraud

In United States v. De Biasi, 712 F. 2d 785 (2d Cir. 1983), the court explained the element of "intent to defraud." The defendant in this case had been involved in a conspiracy to commit bank and wire fraud through the use of counterfeit credit cards whereby he would receive blank credit card slips from a merchant and, for a fee, imprint the slips with a card number, cardholder name, and cardholder signature using counterfeit credit cards.

The defendant contended that the evidence did not show that he knew or should have known that each counterfeit credit card he produced had a credit limit in excess of the criminal monetary threshold, or that he specifically intended that each card be used in interstate commerce.

The court rejected this contention and affirmed the defendant's conviction. The court held that the "monetary threshold" and "interstate commerce" elements of the statute are solely jurisdictional, and need not be in the mind of a defendant who knowingly joins a conspiracy where each counterfeit card could in fact be used to obtain over the monetary threshold in goods and services, and would necessarily affect interstate commerce.

Fraudulent Obtainment

One of the most highly litigated elements deals with the construction of the term "fraudulently obtained." In United States v. Kay, 545 F. 2d 491 (5th Cir. 1977), the defendant was convicted of using fraudulently obtained credit cards to acquire goods and services.

On appeal, the defendant argued that the two credit cards in question were not "fraudulently obtained" because the companies would have issued the cards despite the false and misleading statements he made in his applications. The false statements concerned his ownership in a business, his income and his business address.

The appellate court struck down the defendant's argument and upheld as reasonable the jury's finding that the defendant misstated his intention to pay for the charges at the time he applied for the cards. The court also noted that the card issuers would not have issued the cards had they known of the defendant's intent not to pay his debts. The court held that this constituted fraudulent obtainment.

Reliance

It has been held by the courts that criminal fraud requires only proof of "tendency to induce reliance," rather than showing "actual reliance," in order to establish that a credit card was fraudulently obtained.

In United States v. Chapman, 591 F. 2d 1287 (9TH Cir. 1979), the court upheld the defendant's conviction, stating that the phrase "fraudulently obtained" does not require proof of reliance by the innocent party upon false or misleading statements made by the defendant. Here the court struck down the defendant's contention that the bank was aware that his credit application contained false statements and that the bank issued the card despite this knowledge. The defendant had made several false statements on his credit card application that falsely enhanced his financial status. After receiving his credit card, the defendant made charges but failed to make payments for the purchases.

In response to the defendant's argument that proof of actual reliance is necessary to establish that a card was fraudulently obtained, the court noted that criminal fraud required only proof of a "tendency to induce reliance," rather than a showing of actual reliance.

LIMITING YOUR FINANCIAL DAMAGES

Timely Notification

In order to limit your financial damages from the loss, theft and unauthorized use of your credit card, you must notify the card issuer as quickly as possible. Many companies operate a 24-hour toll-free number for cardholders to report lost and stolen credit cards. It is advisable to follow up with a letter. Include the following information: (1) your account number; (2) the date you noticed your card was missing; and (3) the date you first reported the loss. Send the letter by certified mail, return receipt requested, and keep a copy of the letter and the mailing receipt in a safe place until the problem is resolved to your satisfaction.

A sample notification of lost or stolen credit card is set forth at Appendix 4.

Review Statements

In addition to reporting your credit card loss or theft, you should review your subsequent billing statements carefully. If your statements show any unauthorized charges, you must send a letter to the credit card issuer describing each questionable charge. Again, advise the card issuer of the date your card was lost or stolen, and when you first notified them of the loss or theft. Enclose a copy of your notification letter. Send your follow-up letter to the address provided for billing errors. Again, send the letter by certified mail, return receipt requested, and keep a copy of the letter and the mailing receipt in a safe place until the problem is resolved.

Limited Liability Under the Fair Credit Billing Act

Under the Fair Credit Billing Act (FCBA), if you report the loss before the credit card is used, the FCBA provides that the card issuer cannot hold you responsible for any unauthorized charges. If a finder or thief uses your cards before you report them missing, the most you will owe for unauthorized charges is Fifty ($50) Dollars per card. This is true even if a finder or thief uses your credit card at an ATM machine to access your credit card account.

PROTECTING YOUR CREDIT CARDS FROM LOSS, THEFT AND UNAUTHORIZED USE

Credit Card Registration Services

Some companies offer credit card registration services. In return for an annual fee, the company will provide certain services if your credit, ATM or debit cards are lost or stolen, or there is unauthorized use of your card. The company will report the loss or theft to all of the card issuers and financial institutions on your behalf, and will request your replacement cards. This service allows you to make one phone call to the credit card registration company instead of multiple phone calls to each individual card issuer or financial institution.

Although convenient, credit card registration is optional. If you decide to register, you should read the contract carefully to determine the respective rights and responsibilities. For example, determine what your recourse is if the company fails to make the necessary notification, and whether you will be reimbursed for any resulting losses. It is best to compare offers before selecting a credit card registration service as their price, terms and conditions may vary.

FTC Safety Tips

The Federal Trade Commission (FTC) has published the following safety tips for protecting your credit and debit cards:

1. Sign your cards as soon as they arrive.

2. Know where your cards are at all times.

3. Keep your cards in a secure place.

4. Carry your cards separately from your wallet, in a zippered compartment, a business card holder, or another small pouch.

5. Keep your personal identification number (PIN) secret.

6. Do not use PIN numbers that are easily identifiable, such as your address, birthdate, phone number, or social security number.

7. Keep an eye on your card during the transaction, and get it back as quickly as possible.

8. Make sure incorrect receipts are voided.

9. Do not disclose your account number over the phone unless you know you're dealing with a reputable company.

11. Never put your account number on the outside of an envelope or on a postcard.

12. Draw a line through blank spaces on charge or debit slips above the total so the amount cannot be changed.

13. Don't sign a blank charge or debit slip.

14. Tear up carbons and save your receipts to check against your monthly statements.

15. Cut up old cards—cutting through the account number—before disposing of them.

16. Open monthly statements promptly and compare them with your receipts. Report mistakes or discrepancies as soon as possible to the special address listed on your statement for inquiries. Under the Fair Credit Billing Act (FCBA) for credit cards, and the Electronic Funds Transfer Act (EFTA) for ATM or debit cards, the card issuer must investigate errors reported to them within 60 days of the date your statement was mailed to you.

17. Keep a record—in a safe place separate from your cards—of your account numbers, expiration dates, and the telephone numbers of each card issuer so you can report a loss quickly.

18. Carry only those cards that you anticipate you'll need.

19. Don't carry your PIN in your wallet or purse or write it on your card.

20. Never write your PIN on the outside of a deposit slip, an envelope, or other papers that could be easily lost or seen.

21. Carefully check ATM or debit card transactions before you enter the PIN or before you sign the receipt. The funds for this item will be fairly quickly transferred out of your checking or other deposit account.

22. Periodically check your account activity. This is particularly important if you bank online. Compare the current balance and recent withdrawals or transfers to those you've recorded, including your current ATM and debit card withdrawals and purchases and your recent checks. Report any questionable charges promptly and in writing to the card issuer.

23. Notify card companies in advance of a change in address.

24. Don't lend your cards to anyone.

25. If you lose your credit or charge cards or if you realize they've been lost or stolen, immediately call the card issuer. By law, once you report the loss or theft, you have no further responsibility for unauthorized charges. In any event, your maximum liability under federal law is Fifty ($50) Dollars per card.

CHAPTER 6:
EQUAL CREDIT OPPORTUNITY

IN GENERAL

When applying for credit, there are factors a creditor can legally consider in their decision, and those they cannot legally consider. A creditor can consider any factors that shed light on your creditworthiness. Those factors include: (1) Capacity; (2) Character; and (3) Collateral.

Capacity

Capacity refers to your ability to repay the debt. To determine whether you meet these criteria, a creditor will request information concerning your employment, such as your occupation and income. The creditor will also request information about your expenses, debts, and other financial obligations.

Character

Character refers to your willingness to repay the debt. To determine whether you meet this criteria, a creditor will request information about your credit history, such as the amount of debt you owe; how often you incur debt, and whether you pay your bills on time; and whether you are living within your means. The creditor is also concerned with your stability, such as whether you own or rent; how long you've lived at your present address; and the length of your present employment.

Collateral

Collateral refers to security for the debt, such as resources other than your income which will enable you to repay your debt, such as savings, investments or property.

THE EQUAL CREDIT OPPORTUNITY ACT

Due to concerns that the issuance of credit could be a source of discrimination, and that all individuals would not have equal access to credit, the Equal Credit Opportunity Act (ECOA) was enacted in 1972. The ECOA requires that all credit applicants be considered on the basis of their actual qualifications for credit and not be rejected because of certain personal characteristics including: (1) gender; (2) race; (3) marital status; (4) religion; (5) national origin; (6) age; or (7) receipt of public income.

Except for religion, creditors may ask for this information in certain situations, but they may not use it to discriminate against an individual when deciding whether to grant credit. In addition, you cannot be denied credit because you exercised your rights under Federal credit laws such as filing a billing error notice with a creditor pursuant to the Fair Credit Billing Act.

The ECOA protects consumers who deal with companies that regularly extend credit, including banks, small loan and finance companies, retail and department stores, credit card companies, and credit unions. It basically applies to everyone who participates in the decision to grant credit. Businesses applying for credit also are protected by the ECOA.

Selected provisions of the Equal Credit Opportunity Act are set forth at Appendix 5.

AGE

In the past, creditors have denied credit to individuals simply because of their age. Under the ECOA, a creditor may ask your age, but if you are old enough to sign a binding contract, the creditor cannot do the following based solely on age:

1. Refuse to grant you credit;

2. Offer you less credit;

3. Offer you less favorable credit terms;

4. Ignore your retirement income in evaluating your application;

5. Close your credit account;

6. Require you to reapply for credit just because you reach a certain age or retire; or

7. Close your credit account because credit life insurance or other credit-related insurance is not available due to your age.

A creditor may ask your age, and may factor your age in their credit scoring system, but if you are age 62 or older, you must be given at least as many points as a person under 62. The law does allow a creditor to consider certain information related to age, including when you will retire; the amount of credit sought; and how long you will take to repay the debt. Nevertheless, if you have a good credit history over a long period of time, this will be to your advantage, as the creditor must consider all of the factors to determine your creditworthiness. On the other hand, a senior citizen who has no credit history may have difficulty obtaining credit because the credit grantor has no means of determining creditworthiness.

GENDER AND MARITAL STATUS

Under the ECOA, both men and women are protected from discrimination based on gender and marital status, however, the law was originally designed to address the difficulty women historically had in obtaining credit. For example, denying credit or offering less favorable credit terms based on the belief that a woman's income can't be considered because she'll stop work to marry and raise children is unlawful in credit transactions. The general rule is that you may not be denied credit just because you are a woman, or because you are married, single, widowed, divorced, or separated, although in some cases, a creditor may ask whether you are married, unmarried, or separated.

A creditor may not ask your gender on a credit application, or your birth control practices, or whether you plan on having children. In addition, a creditor must consider all of your income, including income from part-time employment, child support, and alimony. Nevertheless, a creditor may consider whether your income is steady and reliable.

Women have the right to their own credit, based on their own individual credit records and earnings, in your own name, as follows:

1. You can choose to use your first name and maiden name; your first name and husband's last name; or a hyphenated last name (Mary Smith-Jones).

2. If you're creditworthy, a creditor may not ask your husband to cosign your account, with certain exceptions when property rights are involved.

3. Creditors may not ask for information about your husband or ex-husband when you apply for your own credit based on your own income unless that income is alimony, child support, or separate maintenance payments from your spouse or former spouse.

Surviving Spouse

Another common scenario occurs when one spouse dies and creditors attempt to close joint credit accounts. Under the ECOA, a creditor cannot automatically close or change the terms of a joint credit card account solely because of the death of a spouse. However, a creditor may require the joint cardholder to update their application or reapply if the joint account was originally based on all or part of the deceased spouse's income, and the creditor has reason to believe the surviving spouse's income alone cannot support the credit line.

When applying for individual credit, the surviving spouse should ask the creditor to consider the credit history of accounts reported in their spouse's or former spouse's name, as well as those reported in their individual name. The creditor must consider this information if the applicant can prove it reflects positively and accurately on their ability to manage credit. For example, the applicant may be able to show through canceled checks that they made payments on an account, even though it's listed in their spouse's name only.

After the re-application is submitted, the creditor will determine whether to continue to extend credit to the surviving spouse, or change their credit limit. The creditor must respond in writing within 30 days of receiving the application. During that time, the surviving spouse can continue to use the account with no new restrictions. If the application is rejected, the creditor must provide specific reasons for the denial, or the applicant's right to obtain this information.

PUBLIC INCOME

Under the ECOA, you cannot be denied credit based on your receipt of public income, such as veteran's benefits, welfare benefits, or social security income. You have the right to have reliable public income considered in the same manner as other income. Nevertheless, a creditor may consider information such as the age of your dependents, because you may lose benefits when they reach a certain age, thus decreasing your income.

REMEDIES

Under the Equal Credit Opportunity Act, you must be notified within 30 days after your application has been completed whether you have been approved or not. If credit is denied, this notice must be in writing and it must explain the specific reasons why you were denied credit or tell you of your right to ask for an explanation. You have the same rights if an account you have had is closed.

If you are denied credit, you should find out why. There may be an error or the computer system may not have evaluated all relevant information. In that case, you can ask the creditor to reconsider your application. The creditor must give you a notice that tells you either the specific reasons for your rejection or your right to learn the reasons, provided you make the request within 60 days of the denial.

If you think you have been discriminated against, cite the law to the lender. If the lender still refuses without a satisfactory explanation, you may contact a federal enforcement agency for assistance or bring legal action. You can also check with your state Attorney General to see if the creditor violated state equal credit opportunity laws. Your state may decide to prosecute the creditor.

If you're denied credit, the creditor must give you the name and address of the agency that regulates that particular creditor. While some of these agencies don't resolve individual complaints, the information you provide helps them decide which companies to investigate. Your complaint letter should state the facts. Send it, along with copies—not originals—of supporting documents.

Following are some of the agencies that handle complaints concerning credit denials based on discrimination.

If your complaint involves a retail store, department store, small loan and finance company, mortgage company, oil company, public utility, state credit union, government lending program, or travel and expense credit card company, contact:

Consumer Response Center

Federal Trade Commission

Washington, DC 20580.

If your complaint concerns a nationally-chartered bank, contact:

Comptroller of the Currency

Compliance Management

Mail Stop 7-5

Washington, DC 20219.

If your complaint concerns a state-chartered bank that is insured by the Federal Deposit Insurance Corporation but is not a member of the Federal Reserve System, contact:

Federal Deposit Insurance Corporation

Consumer Affairs Division

Washington, DC 20429.

If your complaint concerns a federally-chartered or federally-insured savings and loan association, contact:

Office of Thrift Supervision

Consumer Affairs Program

Washington, DC 20552.

If your complaint concerns a federally-chartered credit union, contact:

National Credit Union Administration

Consumer Affairs Division

Washington, DC 20456.

Complaints against all creditors can be referred to:

The Department of Justice

Civil Rights Division

Washington, DC 20530

If you bring a case in federal district court, you can recover damages— including punitive damages—of up to Ten Thousand ($10,000) Dollars. If you prevail, you may also be entitled to compensation for attorney's fees and court costs. If the creditor has engaged in this type of discriminatory action against others, you can join with them and file a class action suit. In that case, if the class action prevails, the class may recover punitive damages of up to Five Hundred Thousand ($500,000) Dollars, or 1% of the creditor's net worth, whichever is less.

CHAPTER 7:
ESTABLISHING, MAINTAINING AND REHABILITATING CREDIT

WHAT IS GOOD CREDIT?

Good credit refers to your financial trustworthiness. It means that your history of payments, employment and salary make you a good credit risk. When you demonstrate good credit, you are usually eligible for lower interest rates and better terms on credit cards and other loan programs. On the other hand, bad credit means you are a financial risk, e.g., because you do not make your payments on time or you borrow an excessive amount of money. If you have bad credit, it is unlikely that you will qualify for a credit card, a mortgage, an auto loan, etc. Prospective employers and landlords also look at your credit history when considering your application.

ESTABLISHING YOUR CREDIT HISTORY

If you are at least 18 years old and have a regular source of income, you may be able to qualify for a credit card, however, a credit card issuer will be reluctant to give you a credit card unless you can establish that you are a not a credit risk. In order to do so, you must have "good credit." Many people who have never obtained credit have no credit history; therefore, one must be established.

There are a number of ways you can begin creating a good credit history: (1) you can apply for a small line of credit from your bank; (2) you can apply for a credit card with a local department store that is willing to extend credit to someone with no credit history; (3) you can apply for a secured credit card—i.e., one that requires you to deposit money in the account first, and lets you borrow against that account; and

(4) you can ask a friend or relative to co-sign a credit card account for you.

However you are able to obtain your first credit card, it is important that you make your payments on time, and that you do not exceed your established credit limit. Once you have demonstrated that you make your credit card payments on time, major credit card issuers are more likely to approve your credit card application.

In order to establish your credit history, your creditors must report to the credit reporting agencies. Although information from most national department store and bank credit card accounts will be included in your report, not all creditors supply information to credit reporting agencies. Certain travel and entertainment card companies, gasoline card companies, local retailers, and credit unions are among those creditors that don't report to credit reporting agencies.

When you review your credit report, you may discover that you still have an insufficient credit file because your creditors do not report your information to the credit reporting agencies and your credit file does not reflect all your credit accounts. If that is the case, you should ask the credit reporting agencies to add this information to your future reports. Although they are not required to do so, they will generally add verifiable accounts for a fee.

MAINTAINING A GOOD CREDIT HISTORY

Maintaining a good credit history is very important. When a consumer applies for credit, such as a credit card or an automobile loan, he or she generally fills out an application that requests information concerning the consumer's creditworthiness. In considering the application, the creditor generally requests a credit report from a credit reporting agency to: (1) verify the information contained in the application; (2) obtain additional information concerning the consumer's ability to take on additional debt; (3) obtain the consumer's credit payment history, e.g. whether the consumer pays debts timely or late; and (4) determine whether there are any unpaid judgments or liens against the consumer that would affect their creditworthiness. A creditor will use the information contained in your credit report to approve or deny your credit application.

The three major credit reporting agencies listed below regularly obtain information from creditors concerning the payment history of its customers. They also search public records for judgment and lien information. When you are unable to pay your debts on time, late payments and other adverse action—such as judgments and liens—will appear on your credit report.

Contact information for the three major national credit reporting agencies is as follows:

EQUIFAX

P.O. Box 740241

Atlanta, GA 30374

Tel: (800) 685-1111

Website: www.equifax.com

EXPERIAN

701 Experian Parkway

Allen, TX 75013

Tel: (888) 397-3742

Website: www.experian.com

TRANS UNION

P.O. Box 1000

Chester, PA 19022

Tel: (800) 916-8800

Website: www.transunion.com

Monitor Your Credit Report Regularly

It is important to monitor your credit report regularly to prevent identity theft and keep your credit file up-to-date. In addition, if you anticipate applying for a credit card, mortgage, auto loan, or other line of credit, you should first obtain a copy of your credit report from each of the three major credit reporting agencies, and inspect the report to make sure all of the information is correct and updated.

The Fair and Accurate Credit Transactions Act

Under the Fair and Accurate Credit Transactions (FACT) Act of 2003, a consumer is entitled to receive a free copy of their consumer disclosure every 12 months from all three major credit reporting agencies. A consumer disclosure refers to all the information in a consumer's credit report that the credit reporting agencies maintain. A consumer disclosure differs from a credit report in that a credit report contains only some of the information in the consumer's credit file.

Under the FACT Act, you are also entitled to receive this information at no charge if you certify to the credit reporting agency that:

1. You are unemployed and intend to apply for employment in the 60-day period beginning on the date you make the certification;

2. You receive public welfare assistance;

3. You believe your file contains inaccurate information due to fraud; or

4. You are a victim of identity theft.

You can request your FACT Act consumer disclosure from one or more of the three credit reporting agencies online, by telephone and by mail, as follows:

Online: Access the website at http://www.annualcreditreport.com/. Follow the instructions on the website.

By Telephone: Call 1-877-322-8228 to request your credit reports by phone. You will go through a simple verification process over the phone, and your reports will be mailed to you.

By Mail: Send your request to the following address:

Annual Credit Report Request Service

P.O. Box 105281

Atlanta, GA 30348-5281

An annual credit report request form is set forth at Appendix 6.

Your Credit Score

It is also helpful to know your credit score. A credit score—also known as a risk score—is an individual consumer's statistically derived numerical value used by a lender to predict the likelihood of certain credit behaviors, including default. Lenders often make credit granting decisions based upon your credit score. In addition to late payments, factors such as your credit card limits and the number of inquiries in your credit file can lower your credit score and lead to a denial of credit. Therefore, it is advisable to find out your credit score prior to applying for credit.

Before the FACT Act was passed, consumers were not given access to their credit score, or the factors that go into determining the score. Under the FACT Act, you may request your credit score, including an explanation of the factors that went into computing your score. The credit reporting agencies are entitled to charge a reasonable fee, as determined by the Federal Trade Commission (FTC), for providing you with this information.

Dispute Erroneous Information

Credit reporting agencies are obligated to make sure the information contained in a consumer's file is current. The rationale for this requirement is to give the consumer a chance to rehabilitate a negative credit history. Maintaining information in this manner is helpful to both the creditor and consumer provided it is accurate, and maintained in a manner so as to protect the consumer's privacy rights.

When reviewing your credit report, make sure all of your personal information is correct, including your name, address, social security number, date of birth, employer, etc. Sometimes credit data get placed on the wrong report, especially if you have a common name, e.g. Mary Jones. This often happens with family members who have the same name, such as John Smith, Sr. and John Smith, Jr.

You should dispute erroneous negative information in your credit report immediately. If you notice any strange item on your report, such as an unauthorized credit card, investigate it immediately. The FACT Act emphasizes the importance of accuracy in consumer credit files. You should contact the fraud department of the credit reporting agency immediately if you believe unauthorized credit accounts have been opened in your name.

A sample letter to a credit reporting agency regarding unauthorized credit accounts is set forth at Appendix 7.

If a consumer disputes the accuracy of information contained in his or her file, the credit reporting agency is required to reinvestigate this information within a reasonable period of time. If, upon reinvestigation, the information cannot be verified, or is proven inaccurate, it must be deleted, and corrected copies must be sent to all parties who recently requested copies of the report.

If an item is changed or removed as a result of your dispute, the credit reporting agency cannot put the disputed information back in your file unless the information provider verifies its accuracy and completeness.

If reinvestigation does not resolve your dispute with the credit reporting agency, you are entitled to include your statement of the dispute in your file and in future reports. Upon your request, the credit reporting agency will provide your statement to anyone who received a copy of the old report in the recent past for a fee.

A sample letter to a credit reporting agency disputing information contained in a credit report is set forth at Appendix 8.

Before the FACT Act was passed, disputes about the accuracy of information in a credit report had to be made directly to the credit reporting agency. Under the FACT Act, a consumer may dispute inaccurate information directly with the company that reported the information, and the company is required to investigate the claim upon notice of the disputed item.

After you have submitted your dispute, you should re-check your credit report in 30 to 60 days to see whether the errors were corrected. If not, continue to dispute the misinformation. If the creditor refuses to remove the negative information from your file, you are entitled to add a statement to each of your three credit reports explaining your position.

REHABILITATING YOUR CREDIT

After you have thoroughly reviewed your credit report, and have had any inaccuracies corrected, you are entitled to an updated copy of your credit report. If you find that your credit report still contains a lot of negative information that is hurting your credit score and preventing you from obtaining credit, you must immediately begin to rehabilitate your credit. In order to improve your credit rating, you should identify those areas that are causing you problems.

Avoid Late Payments

If you often forget to make your payments on time, most lenders have automated payment options that will deduct the payment from your designated bank account in a timely manner. If you use an automated payment option, you will avoid late payment fees and negative information being added to your credit profile.

Reduce High Balances

If your credit score is low because you have high balances on your credit cards, make an effort to reduce your balances. Try to pay more than the minimum payment required. Pay off high interest credit cards first.

Reduce Hard Inquiries

One segment of the credit report that can affect your credit score is the inquiry section. An inquiry is placed in your credit file when someone checks your credit information. A person checking your credit report must have a legitimate business reason to do so, such as a creditor or lender.

If a lender checks your credit for the purposes of approving a credit application, this is called a "hard" inquiry. Too many hard inquiries on your credit report can lower your credit score because lenders may believe you are applying for too much credit and will accumulate debt beyond your ability to pay. You can reduce the number of hard inquiries that appear on your file by limiting the number of credit applications you submit.

If you notice a hard inquiry on your credit report that you do not recognize, contact the business that made the inquiry for more information. If the inquiry was made in error, you can dispute it and have it removed from your credit report. You should also be aware that an unauthorized inquiry might be a warning sign that someone applied for credit in your name and that you could be an intended target for identity theft.

A "soft" inquiry is placed in your credit file when someone checks your credit for a reason other than a credit application, e.g., to determine your eligibility for pre-approved credit offers. A soft inquiry does not affect your credit score.

Remove Expired Information

Negative information can remain in your credit file for a number of years; however, there are expiration dates, as set forth below. Oftentimes, you will find that the credit reporting agency has not removed the negative items by the expiration date; therefore, you should take it upon yourself to review the applicable dates and contact the credit reporting agency if items remain beyond their expiration date.

Bankruptcy

Bankruptcies generally remain on your credit report for 10 years from the date you filed your petition, however, if you filed under Chapter 13 (individual debt adjustment), the item may be removed after 7 years.

Charged Off Accounts

If your account is delinquent and the creditor *tags* it as a "charged off account," this item can remain on your credit report for 7 years.

Closed Accounts

A delinquent closed account can remain on your credit report for 7 years from the date reported. A closed account that was timely paid can remain on your account for more than 7 years.

Collection Accounts

If your account is in collection, it can remain on your credit report for 7 years starting 181 days from the most recent delinquent period preceding the collection action.

Inquiries

Hard inquiries can remain on your credit report for up to 2 years. Soft inquiries do not appear on the copy of your credit report that is provided to companies authorized to check your credit.

Judgments

Judgments generally remain on your credit report for 7 years from the filing date.

Late Payments

If you are between 30 and 180 days late in your payment, this item can remain on your credit report for 7 years.

Tax Liens

An unpaid city, county, state and/or federal tax lien can remain on your credit report indefinitely, however, once the lien is satisfied, it will remain on your credit report for 7 years from the date of payment.

Credit Repair Services

There are companies that claim they can re-establish a good credit rating for the debtor—for a fee—despite how bad one's credit may be. It is generally best to avoid any companies that claim the ability to turn a bad credit report into a good one. The companies who advertise that they can erase bad credit are generally in business to earn a profit by undertaking actions that the individual can handle on their own. For example, if one's credit report includes negative information that is outdated, or contains inaccurate information, the credit-reporting agency, by law, must correct the inaccuracy. It is not necessary to pay someone to have this information deleted. This task can easily be handled by the individual debtor.

If, however, the negative credit report reflects legitimately owed debts, neither the debtor nor a credit repair service would be able to convince a credit reporting agency, or creditor, to report otherwise. Only time, a conscientious effort, and a personal debt repayment plan can improve a poor credit record.

The companies that advertise credit repair services appeal to consumers with poor credit histories. They cannot repair credit and, in fact, their tactics may be illegal and may also engage the consumer in illegal activity, such as asking the consumer to make false statements on credit applications, and fraudulently misrepresenting the consumer's social security number.

According to the Federal Trade Commission, a consumer must be aware of companies that:

1. Want you to pay for credit repair services before any services are provided;

2. Do not tell you your legal rights and what you can do yourself for free;

3. Recommend that you not contact a credit bureau directly;

4. Suggest that you try to invent a "new" credit report by applying for an Employer Identification Number to use instead of your Social Security Number; or

5. Advise you to dispute all information in your credit report or take any action that seems illegal, such as creating a new credit identity.

If you follow illegal advice and commit fraud, you may be subject to prosecution such as mail or wire fraud if you use the mail or telephone to apply for credit and provide false information.

The Credit Repair Organizations Act

Under the Credit Repair Organizations Act, credit repair organizations must give the consumer a copy of "Consumer Credit File Rights Under State and Federal Law" before they sign a contract with the company. In addition, they also must give the consumer a written contract that spells out all of their rights and obligations. The law contains specific protections. For example, a credit repair company cannot:

1. Make false claims about their services;

2. Charge the consumer until they have completed the promised services; or

3. Perform any services until they have your signature on a written contract and have completed a three-day waiting period. During this time, you can cancel the contract without paying any fees.

In addition, the contract must specify:

1. The payment terms for services, including their total cost;

2. A detailed description of the services to be performed;

3. How long it will take to achieve the results;

4. Any guarantees they offer; and

5. The company's name and business address.

Selected provisions of the Credit Repair Organizations Act is set forth at Appendix 9.

THE FAIR CREDIT REPORTING ACT

In response to the inadequacy of the common law remedies for unfair credit reporting activities, Congress enacted the Fair Credit Reporting Act (the "FCRA"). Under the FCRA, creditors may only obtain a consumer's credit report for limited purposes, the most common of which are extension of credit or employment. In addition, a creditor may only request a credit report for the individual consumer involved in the transaction, and cannot obtain a spouse's credit report if the spouse is not a party to the transaction. It is a crime under the FCRA to obtain a consumer's credit report under false pretenses.

If the credit reporting agency willfully or negligently issues a report to a person who does not have a permissible purpose in obtaining the report, the agency is subject to civil liability. An individual credit reporting agency employee who knowingly and willingly issues the report may be subject to criminal sanctions.

The FCRA also requires credit reporting agencies to maintain accurate information, and to permit consumers to correct any inaccuracies found in their reports. However, a credit reporting agency is not subject to civil liability for inaccuracies contained in consumer credit reports provided they "follow reasonable procedures to assure maximum possible accuracy of the information. . ." Nevertheless, if the credit-reporting agency does not follow "reasonable procedures," they may be subject to liability.

A credit reporting agency is liable to the consumer for any actual damages suffered as a result of negligence. Actual damages generally include monetary losses and have also been held to include damages for mental anguish resulting from aggravation, embarrassment, humiliation and injury to reputation, etc. Further, if the violation is willful, punitive damages may also be available to the consumer.

Selected provisions of the Fair Credit Reporting Act are set forth at Appendix 10.

CHAPTER 8:
CREDIT CARD DEBT: MANAGEMENT AND COLLECTION

IN GENERAL

A debt is generally defined as an obligation or liability to pay. A debtor is one who owes a monetary debt to another, known as a creditor. Consumer debt is at an all time high. More people are spending now than ever before, and less are saving. It seems that credit is available to anyone these days, regardless of his or her negative credit rating or lack of income. Over the past 25 years, credit card debt has more than tripled, from approximately $238 billion in 1990 to $755 billion in 2004. Recent statistics show that credit card debt among young Americans has seen the most dramatic rise.

Credit card debt is a type of unsecured debt—i.e., the credit card issuer has no interest in any of the items purchased and has not required the debtor to put up any collateral to secure the debt. Thus, unlike a secured debt, if the debtor defaults on his or her credit card payments, the card issuer has no legal right to repossess any of the goods purchased. Unsecured debt, such as credit card debt, is the most common type of consumer debt.

Credit card debt is also a type of "open-end" credit. Open-end credit—also referred to as revolving credit—allows the cardholder to borrow up to an authorized amount, i.e., the credit limit, on a continuous basis. When you open a credit card account, the credit card issuer will authorize a certain credit limit. If you are trying to establish credit, your initial credit limit will probably be small—e.g., $500. If you make timely payments, your credit limit may gradually increase.

The difference between your credit limit and your outstanding charges is called your available credit. As you incur additional charges, your available credit is reduced. When you make payments, your available credit is replenished.

MANAGING CREDIT CARD DEBT

Credit card debt can quickly become an overwhelming problem. In order to effectively deal with your debt problems, it is important to distinguish between good and bad debt. Credit cards that have high interest rates—i.e., 10% or higher—definitely fall under the "bad debt" column. You should try and pay off these balances as soon as possible, even before you put money away for various savings plans or retirement. It doesn't make sense to put money in a savings account that earns 4% interest, when you continue to pay credit card payments on a credit card that has a 21% interest rate.

To figure out which credit cards to get rid of first, make a list of the bills according to their interest rates. Pay off the cards that have the highest interest rate first. If necessary, it is advisable to use your savings to pay off these high interest credit cards, as you will be able to save much more once these debts are paid.

CREDIT COUNSELING SERVICES

If you need help in dealing with your credit card debt, consider using a credit counseling service. There are nonprofit organizations in every state that advise consumers on debt management. There are also a number of for-profit companies that "claim" to offer free or low-cost credit counseling services; therefore, it is important to do a background check on a company before making an appointment.

A legitimate credit counseling service is generally a nonprofit organization that employs counselors who are knowledgeable about credit and debt collection, who offer their counseling services at little or no cost to consumers. Credit counseling agencies may also offer educational materials and workshops. In addition, universities, military bases, credit unions, and housing authorities often operate nonprofit counseling programs. You should also check with your local bank or consumer protection office to see if it has a list of reputable, low-cost financial counseling services.

The credit counselor acts as an intermediary between the creditor and debtor. The credit counselor helps the debtor prepare a debt repayment plan that is acceptable to both debtor and creditor that pays the debts over a period of time. The counselor is usually able to get the creditor to waive finance and late payment charges so that the debtor need only repay the principal balance due. Once a budget has been established, the debtor generally pays one monthly payment to the service, which apportions the money among the creditors until the debts are paid in full, at which time the accounts are closed. The service usually requires the debtor to surrender all of his or her credit cards in order to be eligible for assistance.

The credit counselor also reviews the debtor's financial picture to help the debtor set up a budget and plan expenses. There is usually no charge for the counseling, however, there may be a charge for managing the debt repayment plan. Some credit counseling agencies charge little or nothing for managing the plan while others charge a monthly fee that could add up to a significant charge over time. You should discuss this early in your meeting to make sure the services offered fit in your budget and will likely have a constructive outcome. Nevertheless, don't expect an overnight change in your situation as a successful repayment plan requires you to make regular, timely payments, and could take 48 months or longer to complete.

A debt repayment plan does not erase your credit history and creditors will continue to report information about the credit card accounts that are handled through a debt repayment plan. For example, creditors may report that an account is in financial counseling, that payments have been missed, or that there are write-offs or other concessions. But a demonstrated pattern of timely payments should help you obtain credit in the future.

DEBT COLLECTION

Debt collection is the process by which the creditor recovers money owed by the cardholder who is either unable or unwilling to pay their debt. When a credit card due date passes with no recorded payment, the creditor's computer starts to churn out late notices, followed by telephone calls, and ultimately—if the amount is considerable—legal action to recover the debt. In the meantime, late fees and finance charges accrue, making it difficult for the debtor to catch up.

Internal Debt Collection Department

The first attempt to collect a debt is undertaken by the internal collection department of the creditor. Initial contacts are made by letter or telephone. Absent success, some debt collectors take increasingly invasive measures to collect the debt. If the creditor is unable to collect the debt voluntarily from the debtor, the creditor's remedy is usually limited to litigation to obtain a judgment against the debtor.

The first contact the debtor may receive from a creditor is usually a form letter—a polite reminder about the past due account. If the debtor doesn't respond with payment, however, the letters continue, with language that gets stronger with each mailing. One should not take these letters personally because they are computer-generated, and the computer can't distinguish one debtor from the next.

A sample Creditor Demand Letter is set forth in the Appendix 11.

The debtor may also receive several phone calls. If the debtor intends to pay the bill, but is unable to do so due to financial constraints, a payment plan can be requested. In the early stages of collection, most creditors are willing to work within the debtor's budget. Make sure that the proposed plan is realistic. It's not going to do much good to enter into a payment agreement and default on it.

The creditor will usually request the debtor to confirm the payment agreement in writing. Generally, a letter setting forth the agreement will be sent to the debtor, requesting that the debtor sign and return the letter. This gives the creditor an advantage if the debtor defaults on the agreement as it provides a written acknowledgement of the debt.

A sample Payment Agreement Confirmation Letter is set forth at Appendix 12.

A successful payment plan should start off slowly, proposing small payments for a number of months, with increases at various intervals. For example, a debtor who owes three hundred dollars on a revolving department store credit card may offer to pay twenty dollars per month for the first three months, increasing to fifty dollars per month for the next three months, etc. In this way, the creditor can see that there is some prospect of recovery in the near future.

The only problem with a payment plan is that the accrual of finance charges, late fees and/or over-the-limit fees often defeats the plan. After a significant number of payments are made, one may find that the principal is the same—if not higher—than when the payments began. Therefore, request that the creditor suspend these charges so all of your payments can be applied to reduce the principal. If so, the likelihood of success with the plan is increased. Some creditors will agree to waive these charges, others will absolutely refuse.

Independent Debt Collection Agencies

Companies usually establish a time period within which they try to collect a debt internally. If these efforts fail, and the creditor is unable to collect the debt or make a satisfactory payment agreement with the debtor, the creditor will generally place the account with an attorney or independent collection agency with whom the creditor contracts.

Independent debt collection agencies generally earn a percentage of any amount they are able to collect. Thus, their business depends on getting money from you. Intimidation is central to their success. They are notorious for using threats, humiliation, misrepresentation, and other forms of harassment to get you to pay. It is important that you remain calm in response to these contacts and know your rights under the law.

There are laws governing debt collection agency conduct with which they must comply or face legal consequences. For example, a debtor has the right to advise the collection agency that he or she no longer wishes any telephone contact concerning the debt. This notice should be in writing, and sent to the collection agency by certified mail with a return receipt requested. If the collection agency continues to make telephone contact concerning the debt, this is a violation, and the debt collector may be held liable for damages.

A sample Notice to Debt Collection Agency to Cease Contact is attached at Appendix 13.

Do not give the collector what he or she wants, which is to scare you into handing over some money. Realize that there is little that they can do, despite the many threats one may read and hear. For example, one common tactic is to continually telephone the debtor. The purpose of these telephone calls is not only to demand payment, but also to try and persuade the debtor to converse and give information that may be helpful in the collection of the debt or enforcement of a judgment.

Some debt collectors request that the debtor provide them with post-dated checks even though the debtor states that their account does not presently have sufficient funds. The debt collector may assure the debtor that the check will not be processed without his or her consent. Don't fall for this routine. The debt collector often employs this tactic so that, if the check is dishonored, he or she can threaten the debtor with criminal bad check prosecution.

Although prosecution for bad checks is unlikely in this scenario, the mere threat can still be unsettling. It is wise not to place oneself in this position in the first instance. In any event, under certain circumstances, using this tactic may expose the debt collector to liability for damages sustained by the debtor.

The debt collector may also threaten immediate legal action to collect the debt. This is unlikely, particularly when they are dealing with a relatively small amount. The costs of litigation are high and often exceed the debt. Using a cost-benefit analysis, it is simply bad business to litigate every bad debt. When the amount is relatively small, most creditors will at some point simply take the loss—also known as a "charge off"—and satisfy themselves with ruining your credit rating.

Further, it is a violation for a debt collector to threaten legal action which is not intended to be taken. Also note that it is illegal for a collection agency to send you a form that appears to be a court document, such as a document resembling an official summons.

Another common tactic some collectors use is to tell the debtor that they are going to "take their home" or "garnishee their wages" if the debt is not paid within a certain amount of time. Despite what you are told by the debt collector, the debt collector cannot immediately "take your home" or actually "collect" any money by attaching your assets or wages, unless they first obtain a judgment.

When you are subjected to abusive collection tactics, simply inform the collector that they are misrepresenting themselves, and that you know your rights. You can even spell it out for them in detail by reciting the applicable law as set forth in the Fair Debt Collection Practices Act (FDCPA) discussed below. Debt collectors dislike communicating with debtors who know their rights and can't be coerced. Ask the debt collector if you can tape the conversation for your records. This will likely intimidate the debt collector, and you may find that he or she actually hangs up the phone on you for a change.

The oppressive and abusive measures that debt collection agencies have been known to take has led to federal and state legislation designed to protect debtors. In addition, there exist a number of common law theories under which an aggrieved debtor can retaliate against unfair debt collection procedures. Thus, it is important to be aware of your rights. If a collector violates your legal rights, you can sue and recover money for your damages. You may even be able to get the debt canceled.

If you are faced with a particularly offensive collection agency, you may also want to notify the original creditor. Most times, the original creditor is unaware of the tactics used by the collection agency with which it contracts. Advise the original creditor that you plan to take legal action, and send a copy of the letter to the appropriate governmental agencies, as well as your attorney. You may gain some satisfaction in knowing that an abusive collection agency loses a client.

The Fair Debt Collection Practices Act

In 1988, the Fair Debt Collection Practices Act (FDCPA) was enacted to supplement the statutory and common law tort remedies available to the debtor to restrain unfair debt collection procedures. The Act contains detailed provisions regulating the manner in which debt collection is carried out. Many state debt collection harassment statutes are patterned after the Fair Debt Collection Practices Act (FDCPA).

A table of state statutes governing debt collection is set forth at Appendix 14.

The FDCPA applies only to debt collection agencies whereas the state statutes modeled after the Act generally apply to creditors as well. Attorneys are not included in the definition of debt collector under the Act.

The Fair Debt Collection Practices Act requires debt collectors to provide information about the alleged debt, and verification of the debt, at the request of the consumer, including the name of the creditor, the amount of the debt, and an offer to provide the name of the original creditor, if different. In addition, a statement must be sent, generally with the first communication, advising the debtor that the debt will be assumed valid if he or she fails to dispute its validity within 30 days. If the debtor disputes the validity of the debt, the debt collector must verify the debt with the creditor.

A debt collector may not contact the debtor if, within 30 days after the debtor receives written notice of the debt, they send the collection agency a letter stating they do not owe the money. However, a collector can renew collection activities if they send proof of the debt, such as a copy of a bill for the amount owed. A debt collector may not apply a payment to any debt the debtor believes they do not owe. If the debtor owes more than one debt, any payment they make must be applied to the debt they indicate as valid.

The Fair Debt Collection Practices Act prohibits various kinds of collection practices, including, but not limited to:

1. Communicating with the debtor at an unusual or inconvenient time or place;

2. Communicating with the debtor at his or her place of employment if the employer prohibits such communications, or if the debtor requests that he or she not be contacted there;

3. Communicating with a debtor who is represented by an attorney;

4. Communicating with third parties without the authorization of the debtor;

5. Communicating with the debtor after he or she has notified the debt collector to cease communication concerning the debt. In this case, the debt collector may not contact the debtor except for the limited purpose of advising the debtor, in writing, of further action to be taken;

6. Making false, deceptive or misleading representations;

7. Using unfair or unconscionable conduct to collect the debt; and

8. Using harassing, threatening or otherwise abusive conduct to collect the debt.

In addition, if the debtor has an attorney, the debt collector must contact the attorney, rather than the debtor. If the debtor does not have an attorney, a collector may contact other people, but only to find out the debtor's address, telephone number, and place of employment. Debt collectors are usually prohibited from contacting third parties more than once. In most cases, the collector may not tell anyone other than the debtor and their attorney that the debtor owes money.

If a debt collector violates any of the provisions of the Fair Debt Collection Practices Act, he or she is liable to the person with whom the violation took place. This would include the debtor and any other persons who were subject to the debt collector's improper tactics. The statute of limitations—the time period within which the action must be commenced—is one year under the Act. A statute of limitations refers to the period within which an action must be commenced by law. Different types of actions carry different time periods.

The debtor is entitled to actual damages, including physical or emotional injury, and actual expenses. The debtor is also entitled to statutory damages of up to One Thousand ($1,000.00) Dollars as set forth in the Act, whether or not actual damages exist, and whether or not the violation was intentional or inadvertent. Debtors who prevail on their claim may also be entitled to legal fees and costs at the discretion of the court.

Selected provisions of the Fair Debt Collection Practices Act are set forth at Appendix 15.

LEGAL ACTION

As stated above, most creditors will not pursue legal action to recover a relatively small debt, particularly if the projected costs of the action outweigh the recovery. However, if the debt is substantial enough to warrant a lawsuit, the creditor may seek to obtain a judgment to recover the debt.

In order to take legal action to recover a debt, however, the lawsuit must be commenced within the applicable statute of limitations. If the statute of limitations has passed, in most cases, the creditor cannot bring legal action against you to recover the debt. The reader is advised to check the laws of his or her jurisdiction concerning the applicable statute of limitations.

If you decide not to answer the complaint within the time required, you will be considered "in default." A default judgment will thereafter be awarded the creditor. Of course, this means that collection can begin in a relatively short period of time following commencement of the action. Thus, it is advisable to contact an attorney if you are served with a summons and complaint.

JUDGMENT ENFORCEMENT

Whether a judgment is awarded as a result of a litigated dispute, a confession of judgment, or a default, the collection procedures are the same. The party awarded the judgment is known as a "judgment creditor" and the debtor is known as a "judgment debtor." As set forth below, there are a number of ways a judgment creditor can collect on a debt.

Restraining Notice

A restraining notice instructs the judgment debtor, or a third party, that he or she cannot transfer or dispose of any assets of the judgment debtor. The restraining notice is not a levy or a lien on the assets. It merely prevents their transfer. Once a creditor acquires a levy or lien on the assets, the sheriff can execute and take the property.

Property Execution

A property execution is generally delivered to the sheriff, or other designated enforcement officer, so that he or she can enforce it. The sheriff will then demand payment and place a levy on the judgment debtor's assets. The type, amount and whereabouts of the debtor's assets should be specified and included with a copy of the execution sent to the sheriff.

The sheriff is obligated to levy any property specifically identified by the creditor so as to avoid dissipation of the assets. The manner in which a levy takes place generally involves delivery of the execution to the custodian of the property, inspection and inventory of the property, and may also involve the physical relocation of the property. Property subject to execution may be sold at a public auction.

Income Execution

When a judgment creditor attaches the debtor's salary, this is commonly known as a wage garnishment. Depending on the jurisdiction, the judgment creditor is entitled to a statutorily prescribed percentage of the debtor's net pay, e.g. ten percent.

Generally, the sheriff will serve the employer with a wage garnishment. The employer must then deduct the statutory amount from the debtor's paycheck and forward it to the sheriff. The sheriff deducts their fees, and sends the balance to the judgment creditor.

The federal government has limited wage garnishment so that no amount may be withheld for any week unless the debtor's disposable earnings exceed thirty times the federal minimum hourly wage as prescribed in the Fair Labor Standard Act in effect at the time the earnings are payable.

Real Property Execution

A judgment creditor may also file a lien against the debtor's home. However, unless the debt is significant, it is not usual for the creditor to proceed with a foreclosure and sale of the home, as this is a costly undertaking. Nevertheless, the mere filing of a lien against one's home is often enough to get a debtor to negotiate a settlement. In any event, the debtor is prevented from refinancing or selling the home until the lien is satisfied.

Satisfaction of Judgment

If a judgment is paid, a satisfaction of judgment and release of lien, if applicable, must be filed with the proper authorities within a certain time period after the payment is made. A copy of the satisfaction of judgment is usually required to be sent to the judgment debtor. If the judgment is paid, in part, a partial satisfaction of judgment may be filed.

The Judgment Proof Debtor

If you are "judgment proof," the creditor has little hope of ever collecting on the debt. "Judgment proof" refers to the status of a debtor who has no assets or wages that can be attached. Public benefits, such as unemployment, public assistance, disability, or social security benefits are generally protected. Also, if there is income—such as wages or pension and retirement benefits—eligible to satisfy a judgment, there are laws that limit the amount that can be taken at any given time.

If it appears that the debtor's financial situation will change in the future, the debtor should be aware that, depending on the jurisdiction, judgment creditors generally have a long time to enforce a judgment and collect the debt, e.g. ten or more years. Once the statutorily prescribed time period ends, the debt is presumed satisfied unless the judgment debtor has acknowledged the debt or made a payment during that period. Either of these actions would extend the time period for collection.

BANKRUPTCY

Bankruptcy is a serious step which may have certain relatively long-term consequences. One must carefully assess his or her financial situation and determine whether bankruptcy is the right course to take given all of the advantages and disadvantages. Bankruptcy provides a new start to individuals who are saddled with consumer debt, such as credit card debt, that they are unable to repay. Bankruptcy provides the debtor a legal method to wipe out a significant amount—if not all—of his or her debts.

Filing bankruptcy gives the debtor some time to rethink his or her financial situation without worrying about a creditor enforcing a judgment. Upon filing the bankruptcy petition, the debtor is granted an "automatic stay," a court order that prevents creditors from taking any further action to collect debts.

The most apparent disadvantage of filing for bankruptcy protection is the serious damage inflicted on the debtor's credit rating. A bankruptcy filing can remain on an individual's credit report for 10 years under the provisions of the Fair Credit Reporting Act.

This negative credit information generally impedes any efforts to obtain credit, e.g. for a home or automobile purchase, for a considerable period of time. However, an individual who is in debt to the degree that he or she is considering filing bankruptcy has more than likely already sustained considerable damage to his or her credit.

If the bankruptcy is successfully completed, the debtor is given a "bankruptcy discharge," an order that releases the debtor from personal liability for certain types of debts. Once the debtor receives the discharge, creditors can no longer take any collection action against the debtor for those debts that are discharged. The debtor is no longer legally responsible for those debts.

APPENDIX 1:
NOTIFICATION LETTER TO CREDIT CARD ISSUER – BILLING ERROR

Date of Letter

By Certified Mail #

Return Receipt Requested

Name of Credit Card Issuer

Address

City, State, Zip Code

Attn: Billing Inquiries

Dear Sir or Madam:

I am writing to dispute a billing error in the amount of [state dollar amount] on my account. The amount is inaccurate because [describe the problem]. I am requesting that the error be corrected, that any finance and other charges related to the disputed amount be credited as well, and that I receive an accurate statement.

Enclosed are copies of [use this sentence to describe any enclosed information, such as sales slips, payment records] supporting my position. Please investigate this matter and correct the billing error as soon as possible.

Sincerely,

John Doe

Enclosures: [List what you are enclosing.]

APPENDIX 2:
THE FAIR CREDIT BILLING ACT
(15 U.S.C. § 1601) – SELECTED
PROVISIONS

TITLE III - FAIR CREDIT BILLING

§ 301. Short Title

This title may be cited as the "Fair Credit Billing Act".

§ 302. Declaration of purpose

The last sentence of section 102 of the Truth in Lending Act (15 U.S.C. § 1601) is amended by striking out the period and inserting in lieu thereof a comma and the following: "and to protect the consumer against inaccurate and unfair credit billing and credit card practices."

§ 303. Definitions of creditor and open-end credit plan.

The first sentence of section 103(f) of the Truth in Lending Act (15 U.S.C. 1602(f)) is amended to read as follows:

"The term, 'creditor' refers only to creditors who regularly extend, or arrange for the extension of, credit which is payable by agreement in more than four installments or for which the payment of a finance charge is or may be required, whether in connection with loans, sales of property or services, or otherwise. For the purposes of the requirements imposed under Chapter 4 and sections 127(a) (6), 127(a) (7), 127(a)(8), 127(b) (1), 127(b) (2), 127(b) (3), 127(b) (9), an 127(b) (11) of Chapter 2 of this Title, the term, 'creditor' shall also include card issuers whether or not the amount due is payable by agreement in more than four installments or the payment of a finance charge is or may be required, and the Board shall, by regulation, apply these requirements to such card issuers, to the extent appropriate, even though the requirements are by their terms applicable only to creditors offering open-end credit plans.

§ 304. Disclosure of fair credit billing rights.

(a) Section 127(a) of the Truth in Lending Act (15 U.S.C. § 1637(a)) is amended by adding at the end thereof a new paragraph as follows:

> "(8) A statement, in a form prescribed by regulations of the Board of the protection provided by sections 161 and 170 to an obligor and the creditor's responsibilities under sections 162 and 170. With respect to each of two billing cycles per year, at semiannual intervals, the creditor shall transmit such statement to each obligor to whom the creditor is required to transmit a statement pursuant to sections 127(b) for such billing cycle."

(b) Section 127(c) of such Act (15 U.S.C. § 1637(c)) is amended to read:

> "(c) In the case of any existing account under an open end consumer credit plan having an outstanding balance of more than $1 at or after the close of the creditor's first full billing cycle under the plan after the effective date of subsection (a) or any amendments thereto, the items described in subsection (a), to the extent applicable and not previously disclosed, shall be disclosed in a notice mailed or delivered to the obligor not later than the time of mailing the next statement required by subsection (b)."

§ 305. Disclosure of billing contact.

Section 127(b) of the Truth in Lending Act (15 U.S.C. § 1637(b)) is amended by adding at the end thereof a new paragraph as follows:

> "(11) The address to be used by the creditor for the purpose of receiving billing inquiries from the obligor."

§ 306. Billing practices.

The Truth in Lending Act (15 U.S.C. 1601-1665) is amended by adding at the end thereof a new chapter as follows:

> "Chapter 4—CREDIT BILLING

§ 161. Correction of billing errors.

(a) If a creditor, within sixty days after having transmitted to an obligor a statement of the obligor's account in connection with an extension of consumer credit, receives at the address disclosed under section 127(b)(11) a written notice (other than notice on a payment stub or other payment medium supplied by the creditor if the creditor so stipulates with the disclosure required under section 127(a)(8)) from the obligor in which the obligor:

> (1) sets forth or otherwise enables the creditor to identify the name and account number (if any) of the obligor,

> (2) indicates the obligor's belief that the statement contains a billing error and the amount of such billing error, and

> (3) sets forth the reasons for the obligor's belief (to the extent applicable) that the statement contains a billing error, the creditor shall, unless the obligor has, after giving such written notice and before the expiration of the time limits herein specified, agreed that the statement was correct:

(A) not later than thirty days after the receipt of the notice, send a written acknowledgment thereof to the obligor, unless the action required in subparagraph (B) is taken within such thirty-day period, and

(B) not later than two complete billing cycles of the creditor (in no event later than ninety days) after the receipt of the notice and prior to taking any action to collect the amount, or any part thereof, indicated by the obligor under paragraph (2) either:

(i) make appropriate corrections in the account of the obligor, including the crediting of any finance charges on amounts erroneously billed, and transmit to the obligor a notification of such corrections and the creditor's explanation of any cage in the amount indicated by the obligor under paragraph (2) and, if any such change is made and the obligor so requests, copies of documentary evidence of the obligor's indebtedness; or

(ii) send a written explanation or clarification to the obligor, after having conducted an investigation, setting forth to the extent applicable the reasons why the creditor believes the account of the obligor was correctly shown in the statement and, upon request of the obligor, provide copies of documentary evidence of the obligor's indebtedness. In the case of a billing error where the obligor alleges that the creditor's billing statement reflects goods not delivered to the obligor or his designee in accordance with the agreement made at the time of the transaction, a creditor may not construe such amount to be correctly shown unless he determines that such goods were actually delivered, mailed, or otherwise sent to the obligor an provides the obligor with a statement of such determination.

After complying with the provisions of this subsection with respect to an alleged billing error, a creditor has no further responsibility under this section if the obligor continues to make substantially the same allegation with respect to such error.

(b) For the purpose of this section, a 'billing error' consists of any of the following:

(1) A reflection on a statement of an extension of credit which was not made to the obligor or, if made, was not in the amount reflected on such statement.

(2) A reflection on a statement of an extension of credit for which the obligor requests additional clarification including documentary evidence thereof.

(3) A reflection on a statement of goods or services not accepted by the obligor or his designee or not delivered to the obligor or his designee in accordance with the agreement made at the time of a transaction.

(4) The creditor's failure to reflect properly on a statement a payment made by the obligor or a credit issued to the obligor.

(5) A computation error or similar error of an accounting nature of the creditor on a statement.

(6) Any other error described in regulations of the Board.

(c) For the purposes of this section, 'action to collect the amount, or any part thereof, indicated by an obligor under paragraph (2)' does not include the sending of statements of account to the obligor following written notice from the obligor as specified under subsection (a) if:

(1) the obligor's account is not restricted or closed because of the failure of the obligor to pay the amount indicated under paragraph (2) of subsection (a) and

(2) the creditor indicates the payment of such amount is not required pending the creditor's compliance with this section.

Nothing in this section shall be construed to prohibit any action by a creditor to collect any amount which has not been indicated by the obligor to contain a billing error.

(d) Pursuant to regulations of the Board, a creditor operating an open end consumer credit plan may not, prior to the sending of the written explanation or clarification required under paragraph (B) (ii), restrict or close an account with respect to which the obligor has indicated pursuant to subsection (a) that he believes such account to contain a billing error solely because of the obligor's failure to pay the amount indicated to be in error. Nothing in this subsection shall be deemed to prohibit a creditor from applying against the credit limit on the obligor's account the amount indicated to be in error.

(e) Any creditor who fails to comply with the requirements of this section or section 162 forfeits any right to collect from the obligor the amount indicated by the obligor under paragraph (2) of subsection (a) of this section, and any finance charges thereon, except that the amount required to be forfeited under this subsection may not exceed $50.

§ 162. REGULATION OF CREDIT REPORTS.

(a) After receiving a notice from an obligor as provided in section 161(a), a creditor or his agent may not directly or indirectly threaten to report to any person adversely on the obligor's credit rating or credit standing because of the obligor's failure to pay the amount indicated by the obligor under section 161(a) (2) and such amount may not be reported as delinquent to any third party until the creditor has met the requirements of section 161 and has allowed the obligor the same number of days (not less than ten) thereafter to make payment as is provided under the credit agreement with the obligor for the payment of undisputed amounts.

(b) If a creditor receives a further written notice from an obligor that an amount is still in dispute within the time allowed for payment under subsection (a) of this section, a creditor may not report to any third party that the amount of the obligor is delinquent because the obligor has failed to pay an amount which he has indicated under section 161(a) (2), unless the creditor also reports that the amount is in dispute and, at the same time, notifies the obligor of the name and address of each party to whom the creditor is reporting information concerning the delinquency.

(c) A creditor shall report any subsequent resolution of any delinquencies reported pursuant to subsection (b) to the parties to whom such delinquencies were initially reported.

§ 163. LENGTH OF BILLING PERIOD.

(a) If an open end consumer credit plan provides a time period within which an obligor may repay any portion of the credit extended without incurring an additional finance charge, such additional finance charge may not be imposed with respect to such portion of the credit extended for the billing cycle of which such period is a part unless a statement which includes the amount upon which the finance charge for that period is based was mailed at least fourteen days prior to the date specified in the statement by which payment must be made in order to avoid imposition of that finance charge.

(b) Subsection (a) does not apply in any case where a creditor has been prevented, delayed, or hindered in making timely mailing or delivery of such periodic statement within the time period specified in such subsection because of an act of God, war, natural disaster, strike, or other excusable or justifiable cause, as determined under regulations of the Board.

§ 164. PROMPT CREDITING OF PAYMENTS.

Payments received from an obligor under an open end consumer credit plan by the creditor shall be posted promptly to the obligor's account as specified in regulations of the Board. Such regulations shall prevent a finance charge from being imposed on any obligor if the creditor has received the obligor's payment in readily identifiable form in the amount, manner, location, and time indicated by the creditor to avoid the imposition thereof.

§ 165. CREDITING EXCESS PAYMENTS.

Whenever an obligor transmits funds to a creditor in excess of the total balance due on an open end consumer credit account, the creditor shall promptly (1) upon request of the obligor refund the amount of the overpayment, or (2) credit such amount to the obligor's account.

§ 166. PROMPT NOTIFICATION OF RETURNS.

With respect to any sales transaction where a credit card has been used to obtain credit, where the seller is a person other than the card issuer, and where the seller accepts or allows a return of the goods or forgiveness of a debit for services which were the subject of such sale, the seller shall promptly transmit to the credit card issuer, a credit statement with respect thereto and the credit card issuer shall credit the account of the obligor for the amount of the transaction.

§ 167. USE OF CASH DISCOUNTS.

(a) With respect to credit card which may be used for extensions of credit in sales transactions in which the seller is a person other than the card issuer, the card issuer may not, by contract or otherwise, prohibit any such seller from offering a discount to a cardholder to induce the cardholder to pay by cash, check, or similar means rather than use a credit card.

(b) With respect to any sales transaction, any discount not in excess of 5 per centum offered by the seller for the purpose of inducing payment by cash, check, or other means not involving the use of a credit card shall not constitute a finance charge as determined under section 106, if such discount is offered to all prospective buyers and its availability is disclosed to all prospective buyers clearly and conspicuously in accordance with regulations of the Board.

§ 168. PROHIBITION OF TIE-IN SERVICES.

Notwithstanding any agreement to the contrary, a card issuer may not require a seller, as a condition to participating in a credit card plan, to open an account with or procure any other service from the card issuer or its subsidiary or agent.

§ 169. PROHIBITION OF OFFSETS.

(a) A card issuer may not take any action to offset a cardholder's indebtedness arising in connection with a consumer credit transaction under the relevant credit card plan against funds of the cardholder held on deposit with the card issuer unless:

(1) such action was previously authorized in writing by the cardholder in accordance with a credit plan whereby the cardholder agrees periodically to pay debts incurred in his open end credit account by permitting the card issuer periodically to deduct all or a portion of such debt from the cardholder's deposit account, and

(2) such action with respect to any outstanding disputed amount not be taken by the card issuer upon request of the cardholder.

In the case of any credit card account in existence on the effective date of this section, the previous written authorization referred to in clause (1) shall not be required until the date (after such effective date) when such account is renewed, but in no case later than one year after such effective date. Such written authorization shall be deemed to exist if the card issuer has previously notified the cardholder that the use of his credit card account will subject any funds, which the card issuer holds in deposit accounts of such cardholder to offset against any amounts due and payable on his credit card account which have not been paid in accordance with the terms of the agreement between the card issuer and the cardholder.

(b) This section does not alter or affect the right under State law of a card issuer to attach or otherwise levy upon funds of a cardholder held on deposit with the card issuer if that remedy is constitutionally available to creditors generally.

§ 170. RIGHTS OF CREDIT CARD CUSTOMERS.

(a) Subject to the limitation contained in subsection (b), a card issuer who has issued a credit card to a cardholder pursuant to an open end consumer credit plan shall be subject to all claims (other than tort claims) and defenses arising out of any transaction in which the credit card is used as a method of payment or extension of credit if:

(1) the obligor has made a good faith attempt to obtain satisfactory resolution of a disagreement or problem relative to the transaction from the person honoring the credit card;

(2) the amount of the initial transaction exceeds $50; and

(3) the place where the initial transaction occurred was in the same State as the mailing address previously provided by the cardholder or was within 100 miles from such address, except that the limitations set forth in clauses (2) and (3) with respect to an obligor's right to assert claims and defenses against a card issuer shall not be applicable to any transaction in which the person honoring the credit card:

(A) is the same person as the card issuer,

(B) is controlled by the card issuer,

(C) is under direct or indirect common control with the card issuer,

(D) is a franchised dealer in the card issuer's products or services, or

(E) has obtained the order for such transaction through a mail solicitation made by or participated in by the card issuer in which the cardholder is solicited to enter into such transaction by using the credit card issued by the card issuer.

(b) The amount of claims or defenses asserted by the cardholder may not exceed the amount of credit outstanding with respect to such transaction at the time the cardholder first notifies the card issuer or the person honoring the credit card of such claim or defense. For the purpose of determining the amount of credit outstanding in the preceding sentence, payments and credits to the cardholder's account are deemed to have been applied, in the order indicated, to the payment of:

(1) late charges in the order of their entry to the account;

(2) finance charges in order of their entry to the account; and

(3) debits to the account other than those set forth above, in the order in which each debit entry to the account was made.

§ 171. RELATION TO STATE LAWS.

(a) This chapter does not annul, alter, or affect, or exempt any person subject to the provisions of this chapter from complying with, the laws of any State with respect to credit billing practices, except to the extent that those laws are inconsistent with any provision of this chapter, and then only to the extent of the inconsistency. The Board is authorized to determine whether such inconsistencies exist. The Board may not determine that any State law is inconsistent with any provision of this chapter if the Board determines that such law gives greater protection to the consumer.

(b) The Board shall by regulation exempt from the requirements of this chapter any class of credit transactions within any State if it determines that under the law of that State that class of transactions is subject to requirements substantially similar to those imposed under this chapter or that such law gives greater protection to the consumer, and that there is adequate provision for enforcement."

APPENDIX 3:
TABLE OF STATE USURY LAWS

STATE	LEGAL RATE	USURY LIMIT
ALABAMA	6%	8%
ALASKA	10.5%	more than 5% above the Federal Reserve interest rate on the day the loan was made
ARIZONA	10%	n/a
ARKANSAS	6%	for non-consumers the usury limit is 5% above the Federal Reserve's interest rate; for consumers the general usury limit is 17%
CALIFORNIA	10% for consumers	for non-consumers the usury limit is more than 5% greater than the rate of the Federal Reserve Bank of San Francisco
COLORADO	8%	45% (general); 12% (consumers)
CONNECTICUT	8%	12%
DELAWARE	5% over the Federal Reserve rate	n/a
DISTRICT OF COLUMBIA	6%	24%
FLORIDA	12%	18% (25% on loans above $500,000)
GEORGIA	7%	16% (loans below $3,000); 5% (loans above $3,000)
HAWAII	10%	12% (consumer transactions)
IDAHO	12%	n/a
ILLINOIS	5%	9%
INDIANA	10%	n/a
IOWA	10%	12% (consumer transactions)

KANSAS	10%	15% (general); 18% (consumer transactions-first $1,000); 14.45% (above $1,000)
KENTUCKY	8%	4% greater than the Federal Reserve rate or 19% whichever is greater; no limit (loans above $15,000)
LOUISIANA	one point over the average prime rate not to exceed 14% nor be less than 7%	12% (individuals); no limit (corporations)
MAINE	6%	n/a
MARYLAND	6%	24%
MASSACHUSETTS	6%	20% (general)
MICHIGAN	5%	7% (general)
MINNESOTA	6%	8%
MISSISSIPPI	9%	more than 10% or more than 5% above federal reserve rate; no limit (commercial loans above $5, 000)
MISSOURI	9%	no usury defense for corporations
MONTANA	10%	above 6% greater than NYC bank prime rate
NEBRASKA	6%	16% (general)
NEVADA	12%	no usury limit
NEW HAMPSHIRE	10%	no usury limit
NEW JERSEY	6%	30% (individuals); 50% (corporations)
NEW MEXICO	15%	n/a
NEW YORK	9%	16% (general)
NORTH CAROLINA	8%	8% (general)
NORTH DAKOTA	6%	5-1/2% above the six-month treasury bill interest rate
OKLAHOMA	6%	10% (unless person is licensed to make consumer loans); 45% (non-consumer loans)
OREGON	9%	12% (loans below $50,000; 5% above discount rate (commercial paper)
PENNSYLVANIA	6%	6% (general for loans below $50,000 except loans with a lien on non-residential real estate; loans to corporations; loans that have no collateral above $35,000

PUERTO RICO	6%	as set by Finance Board of Office of Commissioner of Financial Institutions
RHODE ISLAND	12%	21% (general); 9% (T-Bills)
SOUTH CAROLINA	8.75%	no usury limit subject to federal criminal laws against loan sharking
SOUTH DAKOTA	15%	no usury limit
TENNESSEE	10%	24% or four points above average prime loan rate whichever is less
TEXAS	6%	n/a
UTAH	10%	floating rates (consumer transactions)
VERMONT	12%	12% (general); 18% (retail installment contracts-first $500); 15% (retail installment contracts-above $500)
VIRGINIA	8% multiple regulated rates (consumer loans)	no usury limit (corporations and business loans); exempt (loans over $5000 for business or investment purposes)
WASHINGTON	12%	12% (general) the legal rate is 12% or four points above the average T-Bill rate for the past 26 weeks whichever is greater
WEST VIRGINIA	6%	8% (contractual rate); Commissioner of Banking issues rates (real estate loans)
WISCONSIN	5%	no general usury limit (corporations); the legal rate of interest is 5%
WYOMING	10%	n/a

APPENDIX 4:
NOTIFICATION LETTER TO
CREDIT CARD ISSUER – LOST OR
STOLEN CREDIT CARD

Date of Letter

By Certified Mail #

Return Receipt Requested

Name of Credit Card Issuer

Address

City, State, Zip Code

Attn: Lost Prevention Department

Dear Sir or Madam:

I am writing to follow up on my telephone call placed to your loss prevention department concerning the [loss/theft] of my credit card issued by your Company. It came to my attention that my credit card bearing the account number [insert credit card number] was missing on [date missing]. I subsequently notified the loss prevention department of your Company on [date of notification] as per the instructions in my cardholder agreement.

Please confirm that this account has been closed and that a replacement card has been mailed to me.

If you have any questions or concerns please contact me. Thank you.

Very truly yours,

[Signature Line]

APPENDIX 5:
THE EQUAL CREDIT OPPORTUNITY ACT – SELECTED PROVISIONS

TITLE VII - EQUAL CREDIT OPPORTUNITY ACT

§ 701. Prohibited discrimination; reasons for adverse action.

(a) It shall be unlawful for any creditor to discriminate against any applicant, with respect to any aspect of a credit transaction—

(1) on the basis of race, color, religion, national origin, sex or marital status, or age (provided the applicant has the capacity to contract);

(2) because all or part of the applicant's income derives from any public assistance program; or

(3) because the applicant has in good faith exercised any right under the Consumer Credit Protection Act.

(b) It shall not constitute discrimination for purposes of this title for a creditor—

(1) to make an inquiry of marital status if such inquiry is for the purpose of ascertaining the creditor's rights and remedies applicable to the particular extension of credit and not to discriminate in a determination of credit-worthiness;

(2) to make an inquiry of the applicant's age or of whether the applicant's income derives from any public assistance program if such inquiry is for the purpose of determining the amount and probable continuance of income levels, credit history, or other pertinent element of credit-worthiness as provided in regulations of the Board;

(3) to use any empirically derived credit system which considers age if such system is demonstrably and statistically sound in accordance

with regulations of the Board, except that in the operation of such system the age of an elderly applicant may not be assigned a negative factor or value; or

(4) to make an inquiry or to consider the age of an elderly applicant when the age of such applicant is to be used by the creditor in the extension of credit in favor of such applicant.

(c) It is not a violation of this section for a creditor to refuse to extend credit offered pursuant to—

(1) any credit assistance program expressly authorized by law for an economically disadvantaged class of persons;

(2) any credit assistance program administered by a nonprofit organization for its members or an economically disadvantaged class of persons; or

(3) any special purpose credit program offered by a profit-making organization to meet special social needs which meets standards prescribed in regulations by the Board; if such refusal is required by or made pursuant to such program.

(d)(1) Within thirty days (or such longer reasonable time as specified in regulations of the Board for any class of credit transaction) after receipt of a completed application for credit, a creditor shall notify the applicant of its action on the application.

(2) Each applicant against whom adverse action is taken shall be entitled to a statement of reasons for such action from the creditor. A creditor satisfies this obligation by—

(A) providing statements of reasons in writing as a matter of course to applicants against whom adverse action is taken; or

(B) giving written notification of adverse action which discloses (i) the applicant's right to a statement of reasons within thirty days after receipt by the creditor of a request made within sixty days after such notification, and (ii) the identity of the persons or office from which such statement may be obtained. Such statement may be given orally if the written notification advises the applicant of his right to have the statement of reasons confirmed in writing on written request.

(3) A statement of reasons meets the requirements of this section only if it contains the specific reasons for the adverse action taken.

(4) Where a creditor has been requested by a third party to make a specific extension of credit directly or indirectly to an applicant, the notification and statement of reasons required by this subsection

may be made directly by such creditor, or indirectly through the third party, provided in either case that the identity of the creditor is disclosed.

(5) The requirements of paragraph (2), (3), or (4) may be satisfied by verbal statements or notifications in the case of any creditor who did not act on more than one hundred and fifty applications during the calendar year preceding the calendar year in which the adverse action is taken, as determined under regulations of the Board.

(6) For purposes of this subsection, the term "adverse action" means a denial or revocation of credit, a change in the terms of an existing credit arrangement, or a refusal to grant credit in substantially the amount or on substantially the terms requested. Such term does not include a refusal to extend additional credit under an existing credit arrangement where the applicant is delinquent or otherwise in default, or where such additional credit would exceed a previously established credit limit.

(e) Each creditor shall promptly furnish an applicant, upon written request by the applicant made within a reasonable period of time of the application, a copy of the appraisal report used in connection with the applicant's application for a loan that is or would have been secured by a lien on residential real property. The creditor may require the applicant to reimburse the creditor for the cost of the appraisal.

§ 702. Definitions.

(a) The definitions and rules of construction set forth in this section are applicable for the purposes of this title.

(b) The term "applicant" means any person who applies to a creditor directly for an extension, renewal, or continuation of credit, or applies to a creditor indirectly by use of an existing credit plan for an amount exceeding a previously established credit limit.

(c) The term "Board" refers to the Board of Governors of the Federal Reserve System.

(d) The term "credit" means the right granted by a creditor to a debtor to defer payment of debt or to incur debts and defer its payment or to purchase property or services and defer payment therefor.

(e) The term "creditor" means any person who regularly extends, renews, or continues credit; any person who regularly arranges for the extension, renewal, or continuation of credit; or any assignee of an original creditor who participates in the decision to extend, renew, or continue credit.

(f) The term "person" means a natural person, a corporation, government or governmental subdivision or agency, trust, estate, partnership, cooperative, or association.

(g) Any reference to any requirement imposed under this title or any provision thereof includes reference to the regulations of the Board under this title or the provision thereof in question.

§ 703. Regulations.

(a)(1) The Board shall prescribe regulations to carry out the purposes of this title. These regulations may contain but are not limited to such classifications, differentiation, or other provision, and may provide for such adjustments and exceptions for any class of transactions, as in the judgment of the Board are necessary or proper to effectuate the purposes of this title, to prevent circumvention or evasion thereof, or to facilitate or substantiate compliance therewith.

(2) Such regulations may exempt from the provisions of this title any class of transactions that are not primarily for personal, family, or household purposes, or business or commercial loans made available by a financial institution, except that a particular type within a class of such transactions may be exempted if the Board determines, after making an express finding that the application of this title or of any provision of this title of such transaction would not contribute substantially to effecting the purposes of this title.

(3) An exemption granted pursuant to paragraph (2) shall be for no longer than five years and shall be extended only if the Board makes a subsequent determination, in the manner described by such paragraph, that such exemption remains appropriate.

(4) Pursuant to Board regulations, entities making business or commercial loans shall maintain such records or other data relating to such loans as may be necessary to evidence compliance with this subsection or enforce any action pursuant to the authority of this Act. In no event shall such records or data be maintained for a period of less than one year. The Board shall promulgate regulations to implement this paragraph in the manner prescribed by chapter 5 of title 5, United States Code.

(5) The Board shall provide in regulations that an applicant for a business or commercial loan shall be provided a written notice of such applicant's right to receive a written statement of the reasons for the denial of such loan.

(b) Consumer Advisory Council

The Board shall establish a Consumer Advisory Council to advise and consult with it in the exercise of its functions under this chapter and to advise and consult with it concerning other consumer related matters it may place before the Council. In appointing the members of the Council, the Board shall seek to achieve a fair representation of the interests of creditors and consumers. The Council shall meet from time to time at the call of the Board. Members of the Council who are not regular full-time employees of the United States shall, while attending meetings of such Council, be entitled to receive compensation at a rate fixed by the Board, but not exceeding $100 per day, including travel time. Such members may be allowed travel expenses, including transportation and subsistence, while away from their homes or regular place of business.

§ 704. Administrative enforcement.

(a) Compliance with the requirements imposed under this title shall be enforced under:

(1) section 8 of the Federal Deposit Insurance Act, in the case of—

(A) national banks, and Federal branches and Federal agencies of foreign banks, by the Office of the Comptroller of the Currency;

(B) member banks of the Federal Reserve System (other than national banks), branches and agencies of foreign banks (other than Federal branches, Federal agencies, and insured State branches of foreign banks), commercial lending companies owned or controlled by foreign banks, and organizations operating under section 25 or 25(a) of the Federal Reserve Act, by the Board of Governors of the Federal Reserve System; and

(C) banks insured by the Federal Deposit Insurance Corporation (other than members of the Federal Reserve System) and insured State branches of foreign banks, by the Board of Directors of the Federal Deposit Insurance Corporation;

(2) Section 8 of the Federal Deposit Insurance Act, by the Director of the Office of Thrift Supervision, in the case of a savings association the deposits of which are insured by the Federal Deposit Insurance Corporation.

(3) The Federal Credit Union Act, by the Administrator of the National Credit Union Administration with respect to any Federal Credit Union.

(4) The Acts to regulate commerce, by the Secretary of Transportation, with respect to all carriers subject to the jurisdiction of the Surface Transportation Board.

(5) The Federal Aviation Act of 1958, by the Civil Aeronautics Board with respect to any carrier or foreign air carrier subject to that Act.

(6) The Packers and Stockyards Act, 1921 (except as provided in section 406 of that Act), by the Secretary of Agriculture with respect to any activities subject to that Act.

(7) The Farm Credit Act of 1971, by the Farm Credit Administration with respect to any Federal land bank, Federal land bank association, Federal intermediate credit bank, and production credit association;

(8) The Securities Exchange Act of 1934, by the Securities and Exchange Commission with respect to brokers and dealers; and

(9) The Small Business Investment Act of 1958, by the Small Business Administration, with respect to small business investment companies.

(b) For the purpose of the exercise by any agency referred to in subsection (a) of its powers under any Act referred to in that subsection, a violation of any requirement imposed under this title shall be deemed to be a violation of a requirement imposed under that Act. In addition to its powers under any provision of law specifically referred to in subsection (a), each of the agencies referred to in that subsection may exercise for the purpose of enforcing compliance with any requirement imposed under this title, any other authority conferred on it by law. The exercise of the authorities of any of the agencies referred to in subsection (a) for the purpose of enforcing compliance with any requirement imposed under this title shall in no way preclude the exercise of such authorities for the purpose of enforcing compliance with any other provision of law not relating to the prohibition of discrimination on the basis of sex or marital status with respect to any aspect of a credit transaction.

(c) Except to the extent that enforcement of the requirements imposed under this title is specifically committed to some other Government agency under subsection (a), the Federal Trade Commission shall enforce such requirements. For the purpose of the exercise by the Federal Trade Commission of its functions and powers under the Federal Trade Commission Act, a violation of any requirement imposed under this title shall be deemed a violation of a requirement imposed under that Act. All of the functions and powers of the Federal Trade Commission under the Federal Trade Commission Act are available to the Commission to enforce compliance by any person with the requirements imposed under this title, irrespective of whether that person is engaged in commerce or meets any other jurisdictional tests in the Federal Trade Commission Act, including the power to enforce any Federal Reserve Board regulation promulgated under this title in the same manner as if the violation had been a violation of a Federal Trade Commission trade regulation rule.

(d) The authority of the Board to issue regulations under this title does not impair the authority of any other agency designated in this section to make rules respecting its own procedures in enforcing compliance with requirements imposed under this title.

§ 704A. Incentives for self-testing and self-correction.

(a) PRIVILEGED INFORMATION.—

(1) CONDITIONS FOR PRIVILEGE.—A report or result of a self-test (as that term is defined by regulations of the Board) shall be considered to be privileged under paragraph (2) if a creditor—

(A) conducts, or authorizes an independent third party to conduct, a self-test of any aspect of a credit transaction by a creditor, in order to determine the level or effectiveness of compliance with this title by the creditor; and

(B) has identified any possible violation of this title by the creditor and has taken, or is taking, appropriate corrective action to address any such possible violation.

(2) PRIVILEGED SELF-TEST.—If a creditor meets the conditions specified in subparagraphs (A) and (B) of paragraph (1) with respect to a self-test described in that paragraph, any report or results of that self-test—

(A) shall be privileged; and

(B) may not be obtained or used by any applicant, department, or agency in any—

(i) proceeding or civil action in which one or more violations of this title are alleged; or

(ii) examination or investigation relating to compliance with this title.

(b) RESULTS OF SELF-TESTING.—

(1) IN GENERAL.—No provision of this section may be construed to prevent an applicant, department, or agency from obtaining or using a report or results of any self-test in any proceeding or civil action in which a violation of this title is alleged, or in any examination or investigation of compliance with this title if—

(A) the creditor or any person with lawful access to the report or results—

(i) voluntarily releases or discloses all, or any part of, the report or results to the applicant, department, or agency, or to the general public; or

(ii) refers to or describes the report or results as a defense to charges of violations of this title against the creditor to whom the self-test relates; or

(B) the report or results are sought in conjunction with an adjudication or admission of a violation of this title for the sole purpose of determining an appropriate penalty or remedy.

(2) Disclosure for determination of penalty or remedy.—Any report or results of a self-test that are disclosed for the purpose specified in paragraph (1)(B)—

(A) shall be used only for the particular proceeding in which the adjudication or admission referred to in paragraph (1)(B) is made; and

(B) may not be used in any other action or proceeding.

(c) ADJUDICATION.—An applicant, department, or agency that challenges a privilege asserted under this section may seek a determination of the existence and application of that privilege in—

(1) a court of competent jurisdiction; or

(2) an administrative law proceeding with appropriate jurisdiction.

§ 705. Relation to State laws.

(a) A request for the signature of both parties to a marriage for the purpose of creating a valid lien, passing clear title, waiving inchoate rights to property, or assigning earnings, shall not constitute discrimination under this title: Provided, however, That this provision shall not be construed to permit a creditor to take sex or marital status into account in connection with the evaluation of creditworthiness of any applicant.

(b) Consideration or application of State property laws directly or indirectly affecting creditworthiness shall not constitute discrimination for purposes of this title.

(c) Any provision of State law which prohibits the separate extension of consumer credit to each party to a marriage shall not apply in any case where each party to a marriage voluntarily applies for separate credit from the same creditor: Provided, That in any case where such a State law is so preempted, each party to the marriage shall be solely responsible for the debt so contracted.

(d) When each party to a marriage separately and voluntarily applies for and obtains separate credit accounts with the same creditor, those accounts shall not be aggregated or otherwise combined for purposes of determining permissible finance charges or permissible loan ceilings under the laws of any State or of the United States.

(e) Where the same act or omission constitutes a violation of this title and of applicable State law, a person aggrieved by such conduct may bring a legal action to recover monetary damages either under this title or under such State law, but not both. This election of remedies shall not apply to court actions in which the relief sought does not include monetary damages or to administrative actions.

(f) This title does not annul, alter, or affect, or exempt any peron subject to the provisions of this title from complying with, the laws of any State with respect to credit discrimination, except to the extent that those laws are inconsistent with any provision of this title, and then only to the extent of the inconsistency. The Board is authorized to determine whether such inconsistencies exist. The Board may not determine that any State law is inconsistent with any provision of this title if the Board determines that such law gives greater protection to the applicant.

(g) The Board shall by regulation exempt from the requirements of sections 701 and 702 of this title any class of credit transactions within any State if it determines that under the law of that State that class of transactions is subject to requirements substantially similar to those imposed under this title or that such law gives greater protection to the applicant, and that there is adequate provision for enforcement. Failure to comply with any requirement of such State law in any transaction so exempted shall constitute a violation of this title for the purposes of section 706.

§ 706. Civil liability.

(a) Any creditor who fails to comply with any requirement imposed under this title shall be liable to the aggrieved applicant for any actual damages subtained by such applicant acting either in an individual capacity or as a member of a class.

(b) Any creditor, other than a government or governmental subdivision or agency, who fails to comply with any requirement imposed under this title shall be liable to the aggrieved applicant for punitive damages in an amount not greater than $10,000, in addition to any actual damages provided in subsection (a), except that in the case of a class action the total recovery under this subsection shall not exceed the lesser of $500,000 or 1 per centum of the net worth of the creditor. In determining the amount of such damages in any action, the court shall consider, among other relevant factors, the amount of any actual damages awarded, the frequency and persistence of failures of compliance by the creditor, the resources of the creditor, the number of persons adversely affected, and the extent to which the creditor's failure of compliance was intentional.

(c) Upon application by an aggrieved applicant, the appropriate United States district court or any other court of competent jurisdiction may grant such equitable and declaratory relief as is necessary to enforce the requirements imposed under this title.

(d) In the case of any successful action under subsection (a), (b), or (c), the costs of the action, together with a reasonable attorney's fee as determined by the court, shall be added to any damages awarded by the court under such subsection.

(e) No provision of this title imposing liability shall apply to any act done or omitted in good faith in conformity with any official rule, regulation, or interpretation thereof by the Board or in conformity with any interpretation or approval by an official or employee of the Federal Reserve System duly authorized by the Board to issue such interpretations or approvals under such procedures as the Board may prescribe therefor, notwithstanding that after such act or omission has occurred, such rule, regulation, interpretation, or approval is amended, rescinded, or determined by judicial or other authority to be invalid for any reason.

(f) Any action under this section may be brought in the appropriate United States district court without regard to the amount in controversy, or in any other court of competent jurisdiction. No such action shall be brought later than two years from the date of the occurrence of the violation, except that—

(1) whenever any agency having responsibility for administrative enforcement under section 704 commences an enforcement proceeding within two years from the date of the occurrence of the violation,

(2) whenever the Attorney General commences a civil action under this section within two years from the date of the occurrence of the violation, then any applicant who has been a victim of the discrimination which is the subject of such proceeding or civil action may bring an action under this section not later than one year after the commencement of that proceeding or action.

(g) The agencies having responsibility for administrative enforcement under section 704, if unable to obtain compliance with section 701, are authorized to refer the matter to the Attorney General with a recommendation that an appropriate civil action be instituted. Each agency referred to in paragraphs (1), (2), and (3) of section 704(a) shall refer the matter to the Attorney General whenever the agency has reason to believe that 1 or more creditors has engaged in a pattern or practice of discouraging or denying applications for credit in violation of section 701(a). Each such agency may refer the matter to the Attorney General whenever the agency has reason to believe that 1 or more creditors has violated section 701(a).

(h) When a matter is referred to the Attorney General pursuant to subsection (g), or whenever he has reason to believe that one or more creditors are engaged in a pattern or practice in violation of this title, the Attorney General may bring a civil action in any appropriate United States district court for such relief as may be appropriate, including actual and punitive damages and injunctive relief.

(i) No person aggrieved by a violation of this title and by a violation of section 805 of the Civil Rights Act of 1968 shall recover under this title and section 812 of the Civil Rights Act of 1968, if such violation is based on the same transaction.

(j Nothing in this title shall be construed to prohibit the discovery of a creditor's credit granting standards under appropriate discovery procedures in the court or agency in which an action or proceeding is brought.

(k) NOTICE TO HUD OF VIOLATIONS.—Whenever an agency referred to in paragraph (1), (2), or (3) of section 704(a)—

(1) has reason to believe, as a result of receiving a consumer complaint, conducting a consumer compliance examination, or otherwise, that a violation of this title has occurred;

(2) has reason to believe that the alleged violation would be a violation of the Fair Housing Act; and

(3) does not refer the matter to the Attorney General pursuant to subsection (g), the agency shall notify the Secretary of Housing and Urban Development of the violation, and shall notify the applicant that the Secretary of Housing and Urban Development has been notified of the alleged violation and that remedies for the violation may be available under the Fair Housing Act.

§ 709. Short title.

This title may be cited as the "Equal Credit Opportunity Act."

APPENDIX 6:
THE ANNUAL CREDIT REPORT
REQUEST FORM

EQUIFAX   **experian**   **TransUnion**

Annual Credit Report Request Form

You have the right to get a free copy of your credit file disclosure, commonly called a credit report, once every 12 months, from each of the nationwide consumer credit reporting companies - Equifax, Experian and TransUnion.

For instant access to your free credit report, visit www.annualcreditreport.com.

For more information on obtaining your free credit report, visit www.annualcreditreport.com or call 877-322-8228.

Use this form if you prefer to write to request your credit report from any, or all, of the nationwide consumer credit reporting companies. The following information is required to process your request. **Omission of any information may delay your request.**

Once complete, fold (do not staple or tape), place into a #10 envelope, affix required postage and mail to:
Annual Credit Report Request Service P.O. Box 105281 Atlanta, GA 30348-5281.

Please use a Black or Blue Pen and write your responses in PRINTED CAPITAL LETTERS without touching the sides of the boxes like the examples listed below:

A B C D E F G H I J K L M N O P Q R S T U V W X Y Z   0 1 2 3 4 5 6 7 8 9

Social Security Number:

Date of Birth:

Month   Day   Year

Fold Here   Fold Here

First Name   **M.I.**

Last Name   **JR, SR, III, etc.**

Current Mailing Address:

House Number   **Street Name**

Apartment Number / Private Mailbox   **For Puerto Rico Only: Print Urbanization Name**

City   **State**   **ZipCode**

Previous Mailing Address (complete only if at current mailing address for less than two years):

House Number   **Street Name**

Fold Here   Fold Here

Apartment Number / Private Mailbox   **For Puerto Rico Only: Print Urbanization Name**

City   **State**   **ZipCode**

Shade Circle Like This → ●

Not Like This → ☒ ⊘

I want a credit report from (shade each that you would like to receive):
○ Equifax
○ Experian
○ TransUnion

○ Shade here if, for security reasons, you want your credit report to include no more than the last four digits of your Social Security Number.

If additional information is needed to process your request, the consumer credit reporting company will contact you by mail.

31238

Your request will be processed within 15 days of receipt and then mailed to you.

Copyright 2004, Central Source LLC

APPENDIX 7:
NOTIFICATION LETTER TO CREDIT REPORTING AGENCY - UNAUTHORIZED ACCOUNTS

Date

Name of Credit Reporting Agency

Address

City, State, Zip Code

Attn: Fraud Department

Dear Sir/Madam:

I am writing to advise you that I am the victim of identity theft. In connection with this crime, it appears that certain credit card accounts were opened in my name using my stolen identity. I obtained a copy of my credit report from your Company and, after reviewing my report, I found that these fraudulent credit card accounts now appear on my credit report, as follows:

[Identify item(s) you claim are fraudulent accounts].

I have also circled these items on the attached copy of my credit report.

I am requesting that the above-listed item(s) and any related derogatory information be removed immediately and that a fraud alert be placed in my file advising creditors that I have been the victim of identity theft and that no new accounts should be opened in my name without contacting me directly and obtaining my authorization.

I have also enclosed copies of the following supporting documentation:

[identify documents which support your position, e.g., police reports or other complaints to government agencies].

Please investigate this matter as soon as possible and make the necessary corrections. I would appreciate if you would send me a copy of the corrected report upon completion of your investigation.

Very truly yours,

[Signature Line]

Enclosures:

[list all attachments]

APPENDIX 8:
NOTIFICATION LETTER TO CREDIT REPORTING AGENCY - ERRONEOUS INFORMATION DISPUTE

[Date]

[Name of Credit Reporting Agency]

[Address]

[City, State, Zip Code]

Attn: Complaint Department

Dear Sir or Madam:

I am writing to dispute the following information contained in my credit file with your Company. The items I dispute are also encircled on the attached copy of the credit report I received from your office, as follows:

Item #1: [Identify item(s) disputed by name of source, such as creditors or tax court, and identify type of item, such as credit account, judgment, etc.] This item is [inaccurate or incomplete] because [describe what is inaccurate or incomplete and why]. I am requesting that the item be deleted [or request another specific change[to correct the information. Enclosed are copies of [use this sentence if applicable and describe any enclosed documentation, such as payment records, court documents] supporting my position.

Item #2: Same as above for any additional disputed information.

Please reinvestigate [this/these) matter(s) and [delete or correct] the disputed item(s) as soon as possible.

Sincerely,

John Doe

Enclosures: [List what you are enclosing]

APPENDIX 9:
THE CREDIT REPAIR ORGANIZATIONS ACT – SELECTED PROVISIONS

15 U.S.C. § 1679. FINDINGS AND PURPOSES.

(a) Findings.—The Congress makes the following findings:

(1) Consumers have a vital interest in establishing and maintaining their credit worthiness and credit standing in order to obtain and use credit. As a result, consumers who have experienced credit problems may seek assistance from credit repair organizations which offer to improve the credit standing of such consumers.

(2) Certain advertising and business practices of some companies engaged in the business of credit repair services have worked a financial hardship upon consumers, particularly those of limited economic means and who are inexperienced in credit matters.

(b) Purposes.—The purposes of this title are—

(1) to ensure that prospective buyers of the services of credit repair organizations are provided with the information necessary to make an informed decision regarding the purchase of such services; and

(2) to protect the public from unfair or deceptive advertising and business practices by credit repair organizations.

SECTION 1679A. DEFINITIONS.

For purposes of this subchapter, the following definitions apply:

(1) Consumer. — The term 'consumer' means an individual.

(2) Consumer credit transaction.—The term 'consumer credit transaction' means any transaction in which credit is offered or extended to an individual for personal, family, or household purposes.

(3) Credit repair organization. — The term 'credit repair organization'—

(A) means any person who uses any instrumentality of interstate commerce or the mails to sell, provide, or perform (or represent that such person can or will sell, provide, or perform) any service, in return for the payment of money or other valuable consideration, for the express or implied purpose of—

(i) improving any consumer's credit record, credit history, or credit rating; or

(ii) providing advice or assistance to any consumer with regard to any activity or service described in clause (i); and

(B) does not include—

(i) any nonprofit organization which is exempt from taxation under section 501(c)(3) of title 26;

(ii) any creditor (as defined in section 1602 of this title), with respect to any consumer, to the extent the creditor is assisting the consumer to restructure any debt owed by the consumer to the creditor; or

(iii) any depository institution (as that term is defined in section 1813 of title 12) or any Federal or State credit union (as those terms are defined in section 1752 of title 12), or any affiliate or subsidiary of such a depository institution or credit union.

(4) Credit.—The term 'credit' has the meaning given to such term in section 1602(e) of this title.

SECTION 1679B. PROHIBITED PRACTICES.

(a) In General.—No person may—

(1) make any statement, or counsel or advise any consumer to make any statement, which is untrue or misleading (or which, upon the exercise of reasonable care, should be known by the credit repair organization, officer, employee, agent, or other person to be untrue or misleading) with respect to any consumer's credit worthiness, credit standing, or credit capacity to—

(A) any consumer reporting agency (as defined in section 1681a (f) of this title); or

(B) any person—

(i) who has extended credit to the consumer; or

(ii) to whom the consumer has applied or is applying for an extension of credit;

(2) make any statement, or counsel or advise any consumer to make any statement, the intended effect of which is to alter the consumer's identification to prevent the display of the consumer's credit record, history, or rating for the purpose of concealing adverse information that is accurate and not obsolete to—

(A) any consumer reporting agency;

(B) any person—

(i) who has extended credit to the consumer; or

(ii) to whom the consumer has applied or is applying for an extension of credit;

(3) make or use any untrue or misleading representation of the services of the credit repair organization; or

(4) engage, directly or indirectly, in any act, practice, or course of business that constitutes or results in the commission of, or an attempt to commit, a fraud or deception on any person in connection with the offer or sale of the services of the credit repair organization.

(b) Payment in Advance.—No credit repair organization may charge or receive any money or other valuable consideration for the performance of any service which the credit repair organization has agreed to perform for any consumer before such service is fully performed.

SECTION 1679C. DISCLOSURES.

(a) Disclosure Required.—Any credit repair organization shall provide any consumer with the following written statement before any contract or agreement between the consumer and the credit repair organization is executed:

"Consumer Credit File Rights under State and Federal Law

You have a right to dispute inaccurate information in your credit report by contacting the credit bureau directly. However, neither you nor any ''credit repair'' company or credit repair organization has the right to have accurate, current, and verifiable information removed from your credit report. The credit bureau must remove accurate, negative information from your report only if it is over 7 years old. Bankruptcy information can be reported for 10 years.

You have a right to obtain a copy of your credit report from a credit bureau. You may be charged a reasonable fee. There is no fee, however, if you have been turned down for credit, employment, insurance, or a rental dwelling because of information in your credit report within the preceding 60 days. The credit bureau must provide someone to help you interpret the information in your credit file. You are entitled to receive a free copy of your credit report if you are unemployed and intend to apply for employment in the next 60 days, if you are a recipient of public welfare assistance, or if you have reason to believe that there is inaccurate information in your credit report due to fraud.

You have a right to sue a credit repair organization that violates the Credit Repair Organization Act. This law prohibits deceptive practices by credit repair organizations.

You have the right to cancel your contract with any credit repair organization for any reason within 3 business days from the date you signed it.

Credit bureaus are required to follow reasonable procedures to ensure that the information they report is accurate. However, mistakes may occur.

You may, on your own, notify a credit bureau in writing that you dispute the accuracy of information in your credit file. The credit bureau must then reinvestigate and modify or remove inaccurate or incomplete information. The credit bureau may not charge any fee for this service. Any pertinent information and copies of all documents you have concerning an error should be given to the credit bureau.

If the credit bureau's reinvestigation does not resolve the dispute to your satisfaction, you may send a brief statement to the credit bureau, to be kept in your file, explaining why you think the record is inaccurate. The credit bureau must include a summary of your statement about disputed information with any report it issues about you.

The Federal Trade Commission regulates credit bureaus and credit repair organizations. For more information contact:

The Public Reference Branch

Federal Trade Commission

Washington, D.C. 20580

(b) Separate Statement Requirement.—The written statement required under this section shall be provided as a document which is separate from any written contract or other agreement between the credit repair organization and the consumer or any other written material provided to the consumer.

(c) Retention of Compliance Records.—

(1) In general.—The credit repair organization shall maintain a copy of the statement signed by the consumer acknowledging receipt of the statement.

(2) Maintenance for 2 years.—The copy of any consumer's statement shall be maintained in the organization's files for 2 years after the date on which the statement is signed by the consumer.

SECTION 1679D. CREDIT REPAIR ORGANIZATIONS CONTRACTS.

(a) Written Contracts Required.—No services may be provided by any credit repair organization for any consumer—

(1) unless a written and dated contract (for the purchase of such services) which meets the requirements of subsection (b) has been signed by the consumer; or

(2) before the end of the 3-business-day period beginning on the date the contract is signed.

(b) Terms and Conditions of Contract.—No contract referred to in subsection (a) meets the requirements of this subsection unless such contract includes (in writing)—

(1) the terms and conditions of payment, including the total amount of all payments to be made by the consumer to the credit repair organization or to any other person;

(2) a full and detailed description of the services to be performed by the credit repair organization for the consumer, including—

(A) all guarantees of performance; and

(B) an estimate of—

(i) the date by which the performance of the services (to be performed by the credit repair organization or any other person) will be complete; or

(ii) the length of the period necessary to perform such services;

(3) the credit repair organization's name and principal business address; and

(4) a conspicuous statement in bold face type, in immediate proximity to the space reserved for the consumer's signature on the contract, which reads as follows: 'You may cancel this contract without penalty or obligation at any time before midnight of the 3rd business

day after the date on which you signed the contract. See the attached notice of cancellation form for an explanation of this right.'.

SECTION 1679E. RIGHT TO CANCEL CONTRACT.

(a) In General. — Any consumer may cancel any contract with any credit repair organization without penalty or obligation by notifying the credit repair organization of the consumer's intention to do so at any time before midnight of the 3rd business day which begins after the date on which the contract or agreement between the consumer and the credit repair organization is executed or would, but for this subsection, become enforceable against the parties.

(b) Cancellation Form and Other Information. — Each contract shall be accompanied by a form, in duplicate, which has the heading 'Notice of Cancellation' and contains in bold face type the following statement:

'You may cancel this contract, without any penalty or obligation, at any time before midnight of the 3rd day which begins after the date the contract is signed by you.

To cancel this contract, mail or deliver a signed, dated copy of this cancellation notice, or any other written notice to (name of credit repair organization) at (address of credit repair organization) before midnight on (date).

I hereby cancel this transaction,

(date)

(purchaser's signature).'.

(c) Consumer Copy of Contract Required.—Any consumer who enters into any contract with any credit repair organization shall be given, by the organization—

(1) a copy of the completed contract and the disclosure statement required under section 1679c of this title; and

(2) a copy of any other document the credit repair organization requires the consumer to sign, at the time the contract or the other document is signed.

SECTION 1679F. NONCOMPLIANCE WITH THIS TITLE.

(a) Consumer Waivers Invalid.—Any waiver by any consumer of any protection provided by or any right of the consumer under this title—

(1) shall be treated as void; and

(2) may not be enforced by any Federal or State court or any other person.

(b) Attempt To Obtain Waiver.—Any attempt by any person to obtain a waiver from any consumer of any protection provided by or any right of the consumer under this title shall be treated as a violation of this title.

(c) Contracts Not in Compliance.—Any contract for services which does not comply with the applicable provisions of this title—

(1) shall be treated as void; and

(2) may not be enforced by any Federal or State court or any other person.

1679H126

CIVIL LIABILITY.

(a) Liability Established.—Any person who fails to comply with any provision of this title with respect to any other person shall be liable to such person in an amount equal to the sum of the amounts determined under each of the following paragraphs:

(1) Actual damages.—The greater of—

(A) the amount of any actual damage sustained by such person as a result of such failure; or

(B) any amount paid by the person to the credit repair organization.

(2) Punitive damages.—

(A) Individual actions.—In the case of any action by an individual, such additional amount as the court may allow.

(B) Class actions.—In the case of a class action, the sum of—

(i) the aggregate of the amount which the court may allow for each named plaintiff; and

(ii) the aggregate of the amount which the court may allow for each other class member, without regard to any minimum individual recovery.

(3) Attorneys' fees.—In the case of any successful action to enforce any liability under paragraph (1) or (2), the costs of the action, together with reasonable attorneys' fees.

(b) Factors to Be Considered in Awarding Punitive Damages.—In determining the amount of any liability of any credit repair organization under subsection (a)(2), the court shall consider, among other relevant factors—

(1) the frequency and persistence of noncompliance by the credit repair organization;

(2) the nature of the noncompliance;

(3) the extent to which such noncompliance was intentional; and

(4) in the case of any class action, the number of consumers adversely affected.

SECTION 1679H. ADMINISTRATIVE ENFORCEMENT.

(a) In General.—Compliance with the requirements imposed under this title with respect to credit repair organizations shall be enforced under the Federal Trade Commission Act [15 U.S.C. 41 et seq.] by the Federal Trade Commission.

(b) Violations of This Title Treated as Violations of Federal Trade Commission Act.—

(1) In general. — For the purpose of the exercise by the Federal Trade Commission of the Commission's functions and powers under the Federal Trade Commission Act [15 U.S.C. 41 et seq.], any violation of any requirement or prohibition imposed under this subchapter with respect to credit repair organizations shall constitute an unfair or deceptive act or practice in commerce in violation of section 5(a) of the Federal Trade Commission Act [15 U.S.C. 45 (a)].

(2) Enforcement authority under other law. — All functions and powers of the Federal Trade Commission under the Federal Trade Commission Act shall be available to the Commission to enforce compliance with this title by any person subject to enforcement by the Federal Trade Commission pursuant to this subsection, including the power to enforce the provisions of this title in the same manner as if the violation had been a violation of any Federal Trade Commission trade regulation rule, without regard to whether the credit repair organization—

(A) is engaged in commerce; or

(B) meets any other jurisdictional tests in the Federal Trade Commission Act.

(c) State Action for Violations.—

(1) Authority of states. — In addition to such other remedies as are provided under State law, whenever the chief law enforcement officer of a State, or an official or agency designated by a State, has reason to believe that any person has violated or is violating this title, the State—

(A) may bring an action to enjoin such violation;

(B) may bring an action on behalf of its residents to recover damages for which the person is liable to such residents under section1679g of this title as a result of the violation; and

(C) in the case of any successful action under subparagraph (A) or (B), shall be awarded the costs of the action and reasonable attorney fees as determined by the court.

(2) Rights of commission.—

(A) Notice to commission.—The State shall serve prior written notice of any civil action under paragraph (1) upon the Federal Trade Commission and provide the Commission with a copy of its complaint, except in any case where such prior notice is not feasible, in which case the State shall serve such notice immediately upon instituting such action.

(B) Intervention.—The Commission shall have the right—

(i) to intervene in any action referred to in subparagraph (A);

(ii) upon so intervening, to be heard on all matters arising in the action; and

(iii) to file petitions for appeal.

(3) Investigatory powers. — For purposes of bringing any action under this subsection, nothing in this subsection shall prevent the chief law enforcement officer, or an official or agency designated by a State, from exercising the powers conferred on the chief law enforcement officer or such official by the laws of such State to conduct investigations or to administer oaths or affirmations or to compel the attendance of witnesses or the production of documentary and other evidence.

(4) Limitation. — Whenever the Federal Trade Commission has instituted a civil action for violation of this title, no State may, during the pendency of such action, bring an action under this section against any defendant named in the complaint of the Commission for any violation of this title that is alleged in that complaint.

SECTION 1679I. STATUTE OF LIMITATIONS.

Any action to enforce any liability under this title may be brought before the later of—

(1) the end of the 5-year period beginning on the date of the occurrence of the violation involved; or

(2) in any case in which any credit repair organization has materially and willfully misrepresented any information which—

(A) the credit repair organization is required, by any provision of this title, to disclose to any consumer; and

(B) is material to the establishment of the credit repair organization's liability to the consumer under this title, the end of the 5-year period beginning on the date of the discovery by the consumer of the misrepresentation.

SECTION 1679J. RELATION TO STATE LAW.

This title shall not annul, alter, affect, or exempt any person subject to the provisions of this title from complying with any law of any State except to the extent that such law is inconsistent with any provision of this title, and then only to the extent of the inconsistenc

APPENDIX 10:
THE FAIR CREDIT REPORTING ACT – SELECTED PROVISIONS

§ 601. SHORT TITLE.

This title may be cited as the Fair Credit Reporting Act.

§ 604. PERMISSIBLE PURPOSES OF CONSUMER REPORTS.

(a) In general. Subject to subsection (c), any consumer reporting agency may furnish a consumer report under the following circumstances and no other:

(1) In response to the order of a court having jurisdiction to issue such an order, or a subpoena issued in connection with proceedings before a Federal grand jury.

(2) In accordance with the written instructions of the consumer to whom it relates.

(3) To a person which it has reason to believe

(A) intends to use the information in connection with a credit transaction involving the consumer on whom the information is to be furnished and involving the extension of credit to, or review or collection of an account of, the consumer; or

(B) intends to use the information for employment purposes; or

(C) intends to use the information in connection with the underwriting of insurance involving the consumer; or

(D) intends to use the information in connection with a determination of the consumer's eligibility for a license or other benefit granted by a governmental instrumentality required by law to consider an applicant's financial responsibility or status; or

(E) intends to use the information, as a potential investor or servicer, or current insurer, in connection with a valuation of, or an assessment of the credit or prepayment risks associated with, an existing credit obligation; or

(F) otherwise has a legitimate business need for the information

(i) in connection with a business transaction that is initiated by the consumer; or

(ii) to review an account to determine whether the consumer continues to meet the terms of the account.

§ 605. REQUIREMENTS RELATING TO INFORMATION CONTAINED IN CONSUMER REPORTS.

(a) Information excluded from consumer reports. Except as authorized under subsection (b) of this section, no consumer reporting agency may make any consumer report containing any of the following items of information:

(1) Cases under title 11 [United States Code] or under the Bankruptcy Act that, from the date of entry of the order for relief or the date of adjudication, as the case may be, antedate the report by more than 10 years.

(2) Civil suits, civil judgments, and records of arrest that from date of entry, antedate the report by more than seven years or until the governing statute of limitations has expired, whichever is the longer period.

(3) Paid tax liens which, from date of payment, antedate the report by more than seven years.

(4) Accounts placed for collection or charged to profit and loss which antedate the report by more than seven years.(1)

(5) Any other adverse item of information, other than records of convictions of crimes which antedates the report by more than seven years.

§ 607. COMPLIANCE PROCEDURES [15 U.S.C. §1681E]

(a) Identity and purposes of credit users. Every consumer reporting agency shall maintain reasonable procedures designed to avoid violations of section 605 [§1681c] and to limit the furnishing of consumer reports to the purposes listed under section 604 [§1681b] of this title. These procedures shall require that prospective users of the information identify themselves, certify the purposes for which the information is sought, and certify that the information will be used for no other purpose. Every consumer reporting agency shall make a reasonable effort to verify the identity of a new prospective user and the uses certified by such prospective user prior to furnishing such user a consumer report. No consumer reporting agency may furnish a consumer report to any person if it has reasonable grounds for believing that the consumer report will not be used for a purpose listed in section 604 [§1681b] of this title.

(b) Accuracy of report. Whenever a consumer reporting agency prepares a consumer report it shall follow reasonable procedures to assure maximum possible accuracy of the information concerning the individual about whom the report relates.

(c) Disclosure of consumer reports by users allowed. A consumer reporting agency may not prohibit a user of a consumer report furnished by the agency on a consumer from disclosing the contents of the report to the consumer, if adverse action against the consumer has been taken by the user based in whole or in part on the report.

§ 609. DISCLOSURES TO CONSUMERS.

(a) Information on file; sources; report recipients. Every consumer reporting agency shall, upon request, and subject to 610(a)(1) [§1681h], clearly and accurately disclose to the consumer:

(1) All information in the consumer's file at the time of the request, except that nothing in this paragraph shall be construed to require a consumer reporting agency to disclose to a consumer any information concerning credit scores or any other risk scores or predictors relating to the consumer.

(2) The sources of the information; except that the sources of information acquired solely for use in preparing an investigative consumer report and actually used for no other purpose need not be disclosed: Provided, That in the event an action is brought under this title, such sources shall be available to the plaintiff under appropriate discovery procedures in the court in which the action is brought.

(3)(A) Identification of each person (including each end-user identified under section 607(e)(1) [§1681e]) that procured a consumer report

(i) for employment purposes, during the 2-year period preceding the date on which the request is made; or

(ii) for any other purpose, during the 1-year period preceding the date on which the request is made.

(B) An identification of a person under subparagraph (A) shall include

(i) the name of the person or, if applicable, the trade name (written in full) under which such person conducts business; and

(ii) upon request of the consumer, the address and telephone number of the person.

(C) Subparagraph (A) does not apply if—

(i) the end user is an agency or department of the United States Government that procures the report from the person for purposes of determining the eligibility of the consumer to whom the report relates to receive access or continued access to classified information (as defined in section 604(b)(4)(E)(i)); and

(ii) the head of the agency or department makes a written finding as prescribed under section 604(b)(4)(A).

(4) The dates, original payees, and amounts of any checks upon which is based any adverse characterization of the consumer, included in the file at the time of the disclosure.

(5) A record of all inquiries received by the agency during the 1-year period preceding the request that identified the consumer in connection with a credit or insurance transaction that was not initiated by the consumer.

(b) Exempt information. The requirements of subsection (a) of this section respecting the disclosure of sources of information and the recipients of consumer reports do not apply to information received or consumer reports furnished prior to the effective date of this title except to the extent that the matter involved is contained in the files of the consumer reporting agency on that date.

(c) Summary of rights required to be included with disclosure.

(1) Summary of rights. A consumer reporting agency shall provide to a consumer, with each written disclosure by the agency to the consumer under this section

(A) a written summary of all of the rights that the consumer has under this title; and

(B) in the case of a consumer reporting agency that compiles and maintains files on consumers on a nationwide basis, a toll-free telephone number established by the agency, at which personnel are accessible to consumers during normal business hours.

(2) Specific items required to be included. The summary of rights required under paragraph (1) shall include

(A) a brief description of this title and all rights of consumers under this title;

(B) an explanation of how the consumer may exercise the rights of the consumer under this title;

(C) a list of all Federal agencies responsible for enforcing any provision of this title and the address and any appropriate phone number of each such agency, in a form that will assist the consumer in selecting the appropriate agency;

(D) a statement that the consumer may have additional rights under State law and that the consumer may wish to contact a State or local consumer protection agency or a State attorney general to learn of those rights; and

(E) a statement that a consumer reporting agency is not required to remove accurate derogatory information from a consumer's file, unless the information is outdated under section 605 [§1681c] or cannot be verified.

(3) Form of summary of rights. For purposes of this subsection and any disclosure by a consumer reporting agency required under this title with respect to consumers' rights, the Federal Trade Commission (after consultation with each Federal agency referred to in section 621(b) [§1681s]) shall prescribe the form and content of any such disclosure of the rights of consumers required under this title. A consumer reporting agency shall be in compliance with this subsection if it provides disclosures under paragraph (1) that are substantially similar to the Federal Trade Commission prescription under this paragraph.

(4) Effectiveness. No disclosures shall be required under this subsection until the date on which the Federal Trade Commission prescribes the form and content of such disclosures under paragraph (3).

§ 611. PROCEDURE IN CASE OF DISPUTED ACCURACY.

(a) Reinvestigations of disputed information.

(1) Reinvestigation required.

(A) In general. If the completeness or accuracy of any item of information contained in a consumer's file at a consumer reporting agency is disputed by the consumer and the consumer notifies the agency directly of such dispute, the agency shall reinvestigate free of charge and record the current status of the disputed information, or delete the item from the file in accordance with paragraph (5), before the end of the 30-day period beginning on the date on which the agency receives the notice of the dispute from the consumer.

(B) Extension of period to reinvestigate. Except as provided in subparagraph (C), the 30-day period described in subparagraph (A) may be extended for not more than 15 additional days if the consumer reporting agency receives information from the consumer during that 30-day period that is relevant to the reinvestigation.

(C) Limitations on extension of period to reinvestigate. Subparagraph (B) shall not apply to any reinvestigation in which, during the 30-day period described in subparagraph (A), the information that is the subject of the reinvestigation is found to be inaccurate or incomplete or the consumer reporting agency determines that the information cannot be verified.

(2) Prompt notice of dispute to furnisher of information.

(A) In general. Before the expiration of the 5-business-day period beginning on the date on which a consumer reporting agency receives notice of a dispute from any consumer in accordance with paragraph (1), the agency shall provide notification of the dispute to any person who provided any item of information in dispute, at the address and in the manner established with the person. The notice shall include all relevant information regarding the dispute that the agency has received from the consumer.

(B) Provision of other information from consumer. The consumer reporting agency shall promptly provide to the person who provided the information in dispute all relevant information regarding the dispute that is received by the agency from the consumer after the period referred to in subparagraph (A) and before the end of the period referred to in paragraph (1)(A).

(3) Determination that dispute is frivolous or irrelevant.

(A) In general. Notwithstanding paragraph (1), a consumer reporting agency may terminate a reinvestigation of information disputed by a consumer under that paragraph if the agency reasonably determines that the dispute by the consumer is frivolous or irrelevant, including by reason of a failure by a consumer to provide sufficient information to investigate the disputed information.

(B) Notice of determination. Upon making any determination in accordance with subparagraph (A) that a dispute is frivolous or irrelevant, a consumer reporting agency shall notify the consumer of such determination not later than 5 business days after making such determination, by mail or, if authorized by the consumer for that purpose, by any other means available to the agency.

(C) Contents of notice. A notice under subparagraph (B) shall include

(i) the reasons for the determination under subparagraph (A); and

(ii) identification of any information required to investigate the disputed information, which may consist of a standardized form describing the general nature of such information.

(4) Consideration of consumer information. In conducting any reinvestigation under paragraph (1) with respect to disputed information in the file of any consumer, the consumer reporting agency shall review and consider all relevant information submitted by the consumer in the period described in paragraph (1)(A) with respect to such disputed information.

(5) Treatment of inaccurate or unverifiable information.

(A) In general. If, after any reinvestigation under paragraph (1) of any information disputed by a consumer, an item of the information is found to be inaccurate or incomplete or cannot be verified, the consumer reporting agency shall promptly delete that item of information from the consumer's file or modify that item of information, as appropriate, based on the results of the reinvestigation.

(B) Requirements relating to reinsertion of previously deleted material.

(i) Certification of accuracy of information. If any information is deleted from a consumer's file pursuant to subparagraph (A), the information may not be reinserted in the file by the consumer reporting agency unless the person who furnishes the information certifies that the information is complete and accurate.

(ii) Notice to consumer. If any information that has been deleted from a consumer's file pursuant to subparagraph (A) is reinserted in the file, the consumer reporting agency shall notify the consumer of the reinsertion in writing not later than 5 business days after the reinsertion or, if authorized by the consumer for that purpose, by any other means available to the agency.

(iii) Additional information. As part of, or in addition to, the notice under clause (ii), a consumer reporting agency shall provide to a consumer in writing not later than 5 business days after the date of the reinsertion

(I) a statement that the disputed information has been reinserted;

(II) the business name and address of any furnisher of information contacted and the telephone number of such furnisher, if reasonably available, or of any furnisher of information that contacted the consumer reporting agency, in connection with the reinsertion of such information; and

(III) a notice that the consumer has the right to add a statement to the consumer's file disputing the accuracy or completeness of the disputed information.

(C) Procedures to prevent reappearance. A consumer reporting agency shall maintain reasonable procedures designed to prevent the reappearance in a consumer's file, and in consumer reports on the consumer, of information that is deleted pursuant to this paragraph (other than information that is reinserted in accordance with subparagraph (B)(i)).

(D) Automated reinvestigation system. Any consumer reporting agency that compiles and maintains files on consumers on a nationwide basis shall implement an automated system through which furnishers of information to that consumer reporting agency may report the results of a reinvestigation that finds incomplete or inaccurate information in a consumer's file to other such consumer reporting agencies.

(6) Notice of results of reinvestigation.

(A) In general. A consumer reporting agency shall provide written notice to a consumer of the results of a reinvestigation under this subsection not later than 5 business days after the completion of the reinvestigation, by mail or, if authorized by the consumer for that purpose, by other means available to the agency.

(B) Contents. As part of, or in addition to, the notice under subparagraph (A), a consumer reporting agency shall provide to a consumer in writing before the expiration of the 5-day period referred to in subparagraph (A)

(i) a statement that the reinvestigation is completed;

(ii) a consumer report that is based upon the consumer's file as that file is revised as a result of the reinvestigation;

(iii) a notice that, if requested by the consumer, a description of the procedure used to determine the accuracy and completeness of the information shall be provided to the consumer by the agency, including the business name and address of any furnisher of information contacted in connection with such information and the telephone number of such furnisher, if reasonably available;

(iv) a notice that the consumer has the right to add a statement to the consumer's file disputing the accuracy or completeness of the information; and

(v) a notice that the consumer has the right to request under subsection (d) that the consumer reporting agency furnish notifications under that subsection.

(7) Description of reinvestigation procedure. A consumer reporting agency shall provide to a consumer a description referred to in paragraph (6)(B)(iii) by not later than 15 days after receiving a request from the consumer for that description.

(8) Expedited dispute resolution. If a dispute regarding an item of information in a consumer's file at a consumer reporting agency is resolved in accordance with paragraph (5)(A) by the deletion of the disputed information by not later than 3 business days after the date on which the agency receives notice of the dispute from the consumer in accordance with paragraph (1)(A), then the agency shall not be required to comply with paragraphs (2), (6), and (7) with respect to that dispute if the agency

(A) provides prompt notice of the deletion to the consumer by telephone;

(B) includes in that notice, or in a written notice that accompanies a confirmation and consumer report provided in accordance with subparagraph (C), a statement of the consumer's right to request under subsection (d) that the agency furnish notifications under that subsection; and

(C) provides written confirmation of the deletion and a copy of a consumer report on the consumer that is based on the consumer's file after the deletion, not later than 5 business days after making the deletion.

(b) Statement of dispute. If the reinvestigation does not resolve the dispute, the consumer may file a brief statement setting forth the nature of the dispute. The consumer reporting agency may limit such statements to not more than one hundred words if it provides the consumer with assistance in writing a clear summary of the dispute.

(c) Notification of consumer dispute in subsequent consumer reports. Whenever a statement of a dispute is filed, unless there is reasonable grounds to believe that it is frivolous or irrelevant, the consumer reporting agency shall, in any subsequent consumer report containing the information in question, clearly note that it is disputed by the consumer and provide either the consumer's statement or a clear and accurate codification or summary thereof.

(d) Notification of deletion of disputed information. Following any deletion of information which is found to be inaccurate or whose accuracy can no longer be verified or any notation as to disputed information, the consumer reporting agency shall, at the request of the consumer, furnish notification that the item has been deleted or the statement, codification or summary pursuant to subsection (b) or (c) of this section to any person specifically designated by the consumer who has within two years prior thereto received a consumer report for employment purposes, or within six months prior thereto received a consumer report for any other purpose, which contained the deleted or disputed information.

§ 615. REQUIREMENTS ON USERS OF CONSUMER REPORTS [15 U.S.C. §1681M]

(a) Duties of users taking adverse actions on the basis of information contained in consumer reports. If any person takes any adverse action with respect to any consumer that is based in whole or in part on any information contained in a consumer report, the person shall

(1) provide oral, written, or electronic notice of the adverse action to the consumer;

(2) provide to the consumer orally, in writing, or electronically

(A) the name, address, and telephone number of the consumer reporting agency (including a toll-free telephone number established by the agency if the agency compiles and maintains files on consumers on a nationwide basis) that furnished the report to the person; and

(B) a statement that the consumer reporting agency did not make the decision to take the adverse action and is unable to provide the consumer the specific reasons why the adverse action was taken; and

(3) provide to the consumer an oral, written, or electronic notice of the consumer's right

(A) to obtain, under section 612 [§1681j], a free copy of a consumer report on the consumer from the consumer reporting agency referred to in paragraph (2), which notice shall include an indication of the 60-day period under that section for obtaining such a copy; and

(B) to dispute, under section 611 [§1681i], with a consumer reporting agency the accuracy or completeness of any information in a consumer report furnished by the agency.

(b) Adverse action based on information obtained from third parties other than consumer reporting agencies.

(1) In general. Whenever credit for personal, family, or household purposes involving a consumer is denied or the charge for such credit is increased either wholly or partly because of information obtained from a person other than a consumer reporting agency bearing upon the consumer's credit worthiness, credit standing, credit capacity, character, general reputation, personal characteristics, or mode of living, the user of such information shall, within a reasonable period of time, upon the consumer's written request for the reasons for such adverse action received within sixty days after learning of such adverse action, disclose the nature of the information to the consumer. The user of such information shall clearly and accurately disclose to the consumer his right to make such written request at the time such adverse action is communicated to the consumer.

(2) Duties of person taking certain actions based on information provided by affiliate.

(A) Duties, generally. If a person takes an action described in subparagraph (B) with respect to a consumer, based in whole or in part on information described in subparagraph (C), the person shall

(i) notify the consumer of the action, including a statement that the consumer may obtain the information in accordance with clause (ii); and

(ii) upon a written request from the consumer received within 60 days after transmittal of the notice required by clause (I), disclose to the consumer the nature of the information upon which the action is based by not later than 30 days after receipt of the request.

(B) Action described. An action referred to in subparagraph (A) is an adverse action described in section 603(k)(1)(A) [§ 1681a], taken in connection with a transaction initiated by the consumer, or any adverse action described in clause (i) or (ii) of section 603(k)(1)(B) [§1681a].

(C) Information described. Information referred to in subparagraph (A)

(i) except as provided in clause (ii), is information that

(I) is furnished to the person taking the action by a person related by common ownership or affiliated by common corporate control to the person taking the action; and

(II) bears on the credit worthiness, credit standing, credit capacity, character, general reputation, personal characteristics, or mode of living of the consumer; and

(ii) does not include

(I) information solely as to transactions or experiences between the consumer and the person furnishing the information; or

(II) information in a consumer report.

(c) Reasonable procedures to assure compliance. No person shall be held liable for any violation of this section if he shows by a preponderance of the evidence that at the time of the alleged violation he maintained reasonable procedures to assure compliance with the provisions of this section.

(d) Duties of users making written credit or insurance solicitations on the basis of information contained in consumer files.

(1) In general. Any person who uses a consumer report on any consumer in connection with any credit or insurance transaction that is not initiated by the consumer, that is provided to that person under section 604(c)(1)(B) [§1681b], shall provide with each written solicitation made to the consumer regarding the transaction a clear and conspicuous statement that

(A) information contained in the consumer's consumer report was used in connection with the transaction;

(B) the consumer received the offer of credit or insurance because the consumer satisfied the criteria for credit worthiness or insurability under which the consumer was selected for the offer;

(C) if applicable, the credit or insurance may not be extended if, after the consumer responds to the offer, the consumer does not meet the criteria used to select the consumer for the offer or any applicable criteria bearing on credit worthiness or insurability or does not furnish any required collateral;

(D) the consumer has a right to prohibit information contained in the consumer's file with any consumer reporting agency from being used in connection with any credit or insurance transaction that is not initiated by the consumer; and

(E) the consumer may exercise the right referred to in subparagraph (D) by notifying a notification system established under section 604(e) [§1681b].

(2) Disclosure of address and telephone number. A statement under paragraph (1) shall include the address and toll-free telephone number of the appropriate notification system established under section 604(e) [§1681b].

(3) Maintaining criteria on file. A person who makes an offer of credit or insurance to a consumer under a credit or insurance transaction described in paragraph (1) shall maintain on file the criteria used to select the consumer to receive the offer, all criteria bearing on credit worthiness or insurability, as applicable, that are the basis for determining whether or not to extend credit or insurance pursuant to the offer, and any requirement for the furnishing of collateral as a condition of the extension of credit or insurance, until the expiration of the 3-year period beginning on the date on which the offer is made to the consumer.

(4) Authority of federal agencies regarding unfair or deceptive acts or practices not affected. This section is not intended to affect the authority of any Federal or State agency to enforce a prohibition against unfair or deceptive acts or practices, including the making of false or misleading statements in connection with a credit or insurance transaction that is not initiated by the consumer.

§ 616. CIVIL LIABILITY FOR WILLFUL NONCOMPLIANCE.

(a) In general. Any person who willfully fails to comply with any requirement imposed under this title with respect to any consumer is liable to that consumer in an amount equal to the sum of

(1) (A) any actual damages sustained by the consumer as a result of the failure or damages of not less than $100 and not more than $1,000; or

(B) in the case of liability of a natural person for obtaining a consumer report under false pretenses or knowingly without a permissible purpose, actual damages sustained by the consumer as a result of the failure or $1,000, whichever is greater;

(2) such amount of punitive damages as the court may allow; and

(3) in the case of any successful action to enforce any liability under this section, the costs of the action together with reasonable attorney's fees as determined by the court.

(b) Civil liability for knowing noncompliance. Any person who obtains a consumer report from a consumer reporting agency under false pretenses or knowingly without a permissible purpose shall be liable to the consumer reporting agency for actual damages sustained by the consumer reporting agency or $1,000, whichever is greater.

(c) Attorney's fees. Upon a finding by the court that an unsuccessful pleading, motion, or other paper filed in connection with an action under this section was filed in bad faith or for purposes of harassment, the court shall award to the prevailing party attorney's fees reasonable in relation to the work expended in responding to the pleading, motion, or other paper.

§ 617. CIVIL LIABILITY FOR NEGLIGENT NONCOMPLIANCE.

(a) In general. Any person who is negligent in failing to comply with any requirement imposed under this title with respect to any consumer is liable to that consumer in an amount equal to the sum of

(1) any actual damages sustained by the consumer as a result of the failure;

(2) in the case of any successful action to enforce any liability under this section, the costs of the action together with reasonable attorney's fees as determined by the court.

(b) Attorney's fees. On a finding by the court that an unsuccessful pleading, motion, or other paper filed in connection with an action under this section was filed in bad faith or for purposes of harassment, the court shall award to the prevailing party attorney's fees reasonable in relation to the work expended in responding to the pleading, motion, or other paper.

APPENDIX 11:
CREDITOR DEMAND LETTER

Date

Mr. John Smith

123 Main Street

White Plains, New York

RE: Charge-A-Lot Account Number 032773

Dear Mr. Smith:

We have been retained by Charge-A-Lot, Inc. to collect the amount of Three Hundred ($300.00) Dollars which is outstanding on your account. To avoid further action, please send a check or money order for the full amount immediately.

Unless you notify us within thirty days after receipt of this letter that you dispute the validity of this debt, we will assume the debt is valid. If within that time period you notify us that you dispute the debt, or any portion of it, we will obtain verification of the debt from the creditor and send it to you, and will provide you with the name and address of the original creditor if it differs from the current creditor.

This letter is an attempt to collect the debt, and any information contained will be used for that purpose.

If you would like to discuss this claim further, please contact the undersigned.

Very truly yours,

Mary Jones, Collection Supervisor

The Pay Now or Else Debt Collection Agency, Inc.

APPENDIX 12:
PAYMENT AGREEMENT
CONFIRMATION LETTER

Date

Mr. John Smith

123 Main Street

White Plains, New York

RE: Charge-A-Lot Account Number 032773

Dear Mr. Smith:

This letter is being sent to you to confirm your agreement to make payments on the above-referenced account so as to avoid further action being taken against you to collect this debt.

As agreed, the outstanding balance of Three Hundred ($300.00) Dollars will be paid in equal monthly installments of Fifty ($50.00) Dollars, beginning on the first of next month, for the next six months until paid in full.

If this letter accurately states the terms of our agreement, please sign where indicated below and return the letter to me in the enclosed self-addressed stamped envelope.

Very truly yours,

Mary Jones, Collection Supervisor

The Pay Now or Else Debt Collection Agency, Inc.

AGREED TO BY:

Signature Line/Date

John Smith, Debtor

APPENDIX 13:
NOTICE TO DEBT COLLECTION AGENCY TO CEASE CONTACT

[Date]

BY CERTIFIED MAIL - RETURN RECEIPT REQUESTED

TO: [The Pay Now or Else Debt Collection Agency, Inc.]

RE: Charge-A-Lot Account Number 032773

Dear Sir/Madam:

This letter shall serve as a notice to your company to cease any further contact with me in connection with the above-referenced account. As I am sure you are aware, the law requires you to comply with this request.

I am presently unable to make payments on this account because [state reasons, e.g., illness, layoff, etc.]. I am trying to reorganize my financial situation, and intend to take care of this matter as soon as I am able. Although I have explained my circumstances to your employees, they have continued to employ collection tactics that are illegal. [Give details]. This has caused me a great amount of stress.

I would appreciate your cooperation so as to avoid having to assert my legal rights in a court of law. Thank you.

Very truly yours,

John Smith

cc: Charge-A-Lot, Inc.

cc: The Federal Trade Commission

cc: The Better Business Bureau

APPENDIX 14:
TABLE OF STATE STATUTES GOVERNING DEBT COLLECTION

STATE	STATUTE
Alabama	Alabama Code §40-12-80
Alaska	Alaska Statutes §§8.24.0.011 et seq.
Arizona	Arizona Revised Statutes Annotated §§32-1001 et seq.
Arkansas	Arkansas Statutes Annotated §617-21-104 et seq.
California	California Civil Code §§1788 et seq.
Colorado	Colorado Revised Statutes §§5-10101 et seq; 12-14-101 et seq.
Connecticut	Connecticut General Statutes Annotated §§36-243.a et seq; 42-127 et seq.
Delaware	Delaware Code Annotated,, Title 30,, §2301(13).
District of Columbia	D.C. Code Annotated §§22-3423 et seq; 28-3814 et seq.
Florida	Florida Statutes §§559.55 et seq.
Georgia	Georgia Code Annotated §§7-3-1 et seq.
Hawaii	Hawaii Revised Statutes §§443-B-1 et seq.
Idaho	Idaho Code §§26-2222 et seq.
Illinois	Illinois Annotated Statutes,, Chapter 111,, §§2001 et seq.
Indiana	Indiana Code Annotated §§25-11-1-1 et seq.
Iowa	Iowa Code Annotated §§537.7101 et seq.
Kansas	Kansas Statutes Annotated §16a-5-107.
Kentucky	None.
Louisiana	Louisiana Revised Statutes Annotated §§9:3510 et seq.
Maine	Maine Revised Statutes Annotated,, Title 32 §§11,001 et seq; Title 9-A §§1.101 et seq.

Maryland	Maryland Annotated Code,, Article 56 §§323 et seq; Maryland Com. Law Code Annotated,, §§14-201 et seq.
Massachusetts	Massachusetts General Laws Annotated,, Chapter 93 §§24 et seq; §49.
Michigan	Michigan Compiled Laws Annotated §19.655; §18.425.
Minnesota	None.
Missouri	None.
Montana	None.
Nebraska	Nebraska Revised Statutes §§45-601 et seq; 45-175 et seq.
Nevada	Nevada Revised Statutes §§649.005 et seq.
New Hampshire	New Hampshire Revised Statutes Annotated §§358-C:1 et seq.
New Jersey	New Jersey Statutes Annotated §§45:18-1 et seq.
New Mexico	New Mexico Statutes Annotated §§61-18A-1 et seq.
New York	New York General Law §§600 et seq.
North Carolina	North Carolina General Statutes §§66-49.24 et seq; 75-50 et seq.
North Dakota	North Dakota Cent. Code §§13-05-01 et seq.
Ohio	None.
Oklahoma	None.
Oregon	Oregon Revised Statutes §§646.639 et seq; 697.010 et seq.
Pennsylvania	18 Pennsylvania Cons. Statutes Annotated §§7311; 201-1 et seq.
Rhode Island	None.
South Carolina	South Carolina Code Annotated §37-5-108.
South Dakota	None.
Tennessee	Tennessee Code Annotated §§62-20-101 et seq.
Texas	Texas Revised Civ. Statutes Annotated,, Arts. 5069-11.01 et seq.
Utah	Utah Code Annotated §§12-1-1 et seq.
Vermont	Vermont Statutes Annotated,, Title 9 §§2451a et seq.
Virginia	Virginia Code Annotated §§18.2 et seq.
Washington	Washington Revised Code Annotated §§19.16.100 et seq.
West Virginia	West Virginia Code §§47-16-1 §§18.2 et seq; 46A-2-101 et seq.
Wisconsin	Wisconsin Statutes Annotated §§218.04; 427.101 et seq.
Wyoming	Wyoming Statutes §§33-11-101 et seq.

APPENDIX 15:
FAIR DEBT COLLECTION PRACTICES ACT – SELECTED PROVISIONS

15 USCS § 1692. CONGRESSIONAL FINDINGS AND DECLARATION OF PURPOSE

(a) Abusive practices.

There is abundant evidence of the use of abusive, deceptive, and unfair debt collection practices by many debt collectors. Abusive debt collection practices contribute to the number of personal bankruptcies, to marital instability, to the loss of jobs, and to invasions of individual privacy.

(b) Inadequacy of laws.

Existing laws and procedures for redressing these injuries are inadequate to protect consumers.

(c) Available non-abusive collection methods.

Means other than misrepresentation or other abusive debt collection practices are available for the effective collection of debts.

(d) Interstate commerce.

Abusive debt collection practices are carried on to a substantial extent in interstate commerce and through means and instrumentalities of such commerce. Even where abusive debt collection practices are purely intrastate in character, they nevertheless directly affect interstate commerce.

(e) Purposes.

It is the purpose of this subchapter to eliminate abusive debt collection practices by debt collectors, to insure that those debt collectors who refrain from using abusive debt collection practices are not competitively disadvantaged, and to promote consistent State action to protect consumers against debt collection abuses.

SECTION 1692A. DEFINITIONS

As used in this subchapter:

(1) The term "Commission" means the Federal Trade Commission.

(2) The term "communication" means the conveying of information regarding a debt directly or indirectly to any person through any medium.

(3) The term "consumer" means any natural person obligated or allegedly obligated to pay any debt.

(4) The term "creditor" means any person who offers or extends credit creating a debt or to whom a debt is owed, but such term does not include any person to the extent that he receives an assignment or transfer of a debt in default solely for the purpose of facilitating collection of such debt for another.

(5) The term "debt" means any obligation or alleged obligation of a consumer to pay money arising out of a transaction in which the money, property, insurance, or services which are the subject of the transaction are primarily for personal, family, or household purposes, whether or not such obligation has been reduced to judgment.

(6) The term "debt collector" means any person who uses any instrumentality of interstate commerce or the mails in any business the principal purpose of which is the collection of any debts, or who regularly collects or attempts to collect, directly or indirectly, debts owed or due or asserted to be owed or due another. Notwithstanding the exclusion provided by clause (F) of the last sentence of this paragraph, the term includes any creditor who, in the process of collecting his own debts, uses any name other than his own which would indicate that a third person is collecting or attempting to collect such debts. For the purpose of section 1692f (6)] of this title, such term also includes any person who uses any instrumentality of interstate commerce or the mails in any business the principal purpose of which is the enforcement of security interests. The term does not include:

(A) any officer or employee of a creditor while, in the name of the creditor, collecting debts for such creditor;

(B) any person while acting as a debt collector for another person, both of whom are related by common ownership or affiliated by corporate control, if the person acting as a debt collector does so only for persons to whom it is so related or affiliated and if the principal business of such person is not the collection of debts;

(C) any officer or employee of the United States or any State to the extent that collecting or attempting to collect any debt is in the performance of his official duties;

(D) any person while serving or attempting to serve legal process on any other person in connection with the judicial enforcement of any debt;

(E) any nonprofit organization which, at the request of consumers, performs bona fide consumer credit counseling and assists consumers in the liquidation of their debts by receiving payments from such consumers and distributing such amounts to creditors; and

(F) any person collecting or attempting to collect any debt owed or due or asserted to be owed or due another to the extent such activity (i) is incidental to a bona fide fiduciary obligation or a bona fide escrow arrangement; (ii) concerns a debt which was originated by such person; (iii) concerns a debt which was not in default at the time it was obtained by such person; or (iv) concerns a debt obtained by such person as a secured party in a commercial credit transaction involving the creditor.

(7) The term "location information" means a consumer's place of abode and his telephone number at such place, or his place of employment.

(8) The term "State" means any State, territory, or possession of the United States, the District of Columbia, the Commonwealth of Puerto Rico, or any political subdivision of any of the foregoing.

SECTION 1692B. ACQUISITION OF LOCATION INFORMATION.

Any debt collector communicating with any person other than the consumer for the purpose of acquiring location information about the consumer shall:

(1) identify himself, state that he is confirming or correcting location information concerning the consumer, and, only if expressly requested, identify his employer;

(2) not state that such consumer owes any debt;

(3) not communicate with any such person more than once unless requested to do so by such person or unless the debt collector

reasonably believes that the earlier response of such person is erroneous or incomplete and that such person now has correct or complete location information;

(4) not communicate by postcard;

(5) not use any language or symbol on any envelope or in the contents of any communication effected by the mails or telegram that indicates that the debt collector is in the debt collection business or that the communication relates to the collection of a debt; and

(6) after the debt collector knows the consumer is represented by an attorney with regard to the subject debt and has knowledge of, or can readily ascertain, such attorney's name and address, not communicate with any person other than that attorney, unless the attorney fails to respond within a reasonable period of time to communication from the debt collector.

SECTION 1692C. COMMUNICATION IN CONNECTION WITH DEBT COLLECTION.

(a) Communication with the consumer generally.

Without the prior consent of the consumer given directly to the debt collector or the express permission of a court of competent jurisdiction, a debt collector may not communicate with a consumer in connection with the collection of any debt:

(1) at any unusual time or place or a time or place known or which should be known to be inconvenient to the consumer. In the absence of knowledge of circumstances to the contrary, a debt collector shall assume that the convenient time for communicating with a consumer is after 8 o'clock antimeridian and before 9 o'clock postmeridian, local time at the consumer's location;

(2) if the debt collector knows the consumer is represented by an attorney with respect to such debt and has knowledge of, or can readily ascertain, such attorney's name and address, unless the attorney fails to respond within a reasonable period of time to a communication from the debt collector or unless the attorney consents to direct communication with the consumer; or

(3) at the consumer's place of employment if the debt collector knows or has reason to know that the consumer's employer prohibits the consumer from receiving such communication.

(b) Communication with third parties.

Except as provided in section §1692b of this title, without the prior consent of the consumer given directly to the debt collector, or the express permission of a court of competent jurisdiction, or as reasonably necessary to effectuate a postjudgment judicial remedy, a debt collector may not communicate, in connection with the collection of any debt, with any person other than the consumer, his attorney, a consumer reporting agency if otherwise permitted by law, the creditor, the attorney of the creditor, or the attorney of the debt collector.

(c) Ceasing communication.

If a consumer notifies a debt collector in writing that the consumer refuses to pay a debt or that the consumer wishes the debt collector to cease further communication with the consumer, the debt collector shall not communicate further with the consumer with respect to such debt, except:

(1) to advise the consumer that the debt collector's further efforts are being terminated;

(2) to notify the consumer that the debt collector or creditor may invoke specified remedies which are ordinarily invoked by such debt collector or creditor; or

(3) where applicable, to notify the consumer that the debt collector or creditor intends to invoke a specified remedy. If such notice from the consumer is made by mail, notification shall be complete upon receipt.

(d) "Consumer" defined.

For the purpose of this section, the term "consumer" includes the consumer's spouse,

parent (if the consumer is a minor), guardian, executor, or administrator.

SECTION 1692D. HARASSMENT OR ABUSE.

A debt collector may not engage in any conduct the natural consequence of which is to harass, oppress, or abuse any person in connection with the collection of a debt. Without limiting the general application of the foregoing, the following conduct is a violation of this section:

(1) The use or threat of use of violence or other criminal means to harm the physical person, reputation, or property of any person.

(2) The use of obscene or profane language or language the natural consequence of which is to abuse the hearer or reader.

(3) The publication of a list of consumers who allegedly refuse to pay debts, except to a consumer reporting agency or to persons meeting the requirements of section 1681a (f) or 1681b (3) of this title.

(4) The advertisement for sale of any debt to coerce payment of the debt.

(5) Causing a telephone to ring or engaging any person in telephone conversation repeatedly or continuously with intent to annoy, abuse or harass any person at the called number.

(6) Except as provided in section 1692b of this title, the placement of telephone calls without meaningful disclosure of the caller's identity.

SECTION 1692E. FALSE OR MISLEADING REPRESENTATIONS.

A debt collector may not use any false, deceptive, or misleading representation or means in connection with the collection of any debt. Without limiting the general application of the foregoing, the following conduct is a violation of this section:

(1) The false representation or implication that the debt collector is vouched for, bonded by, or affiliated with the United States or any State, including the use of any badge, uniform, or facsimile thereof.

(2) The false representation of:

(A) the character, amount, or legal status of any debt; or

(B) any services rendered or compensation which may be lawfully received by any debt collector for the collection of a debt.

(3) The false representation or implication that any individual is an attorney or that any communication is from an attorney.

(4) The representation or implication that nonpayment of any debt will result in the arrest or imprisonment of any person or the seizure, garnishment, attachment, or sale of any property or wages of any person unless such action is lawful and the debt collector or creditor intends to take such action.

(5) The threat to take any action that cannot legally be taken or that is not intended to be taken.

(6) The false representation or implication that a sale, referral, or other transfer of any interest in a debt shall cause the consumer to:

(A) lose any claim or defense to payment of the debt; or

(B) become subject to any practice prohibited by this subchapter.

(7) The false representation or implication that the consumer committed any crime or other conduct in order to disgrace the consumer.

(8) Communicating or threatening to communicate to any person credit information which is known or which should be known to be false, including the failure to communicate that a disputed debt is disputed.

(9) The use or distribution of any written communication which simulates or is falsely represented to be a document authorized, issued, or approved by any court, official, or agency of the United States or any State, or which creates a false impression as to its source, authorization, or approval.

(10) The use of any false representation or deceptive means to collect or attempt to collect any debt or to obtain information concerning a consumer.

(11) The failure to disclose in the initial written communication with the consumer and, in addition, if the initial communication with the is oral, in that initial oral communication, that the debt collector is attempting to collect a debt and that any information obtained will be used for that purpose, and the failure to disclose in subsequent communications that the communication is from a debt collector, except that this paragraph shall not apply to a formal pleading made in connection with a legal action.

(12) The false representation or implication that accounts have been turned over to innocent purchasers for value.

(13) The false representation or implication that documents are legal process.

(14) The use of any business, company, or organization name other than the true name of the debt collector's business, company, or organization.

(15) The false representation or implication that documents are not legal process forms or do not require action by the consumer.

(16) The false representation or implication that a debt collector operates or is employed by a consumer reporting agency as defined by section 1681a (f)] of this title.

SECTION 1692F. UNFAIR PRACTICES.

A debt collector may not use unfair or unconscionable means to collect or attempt to collect any debt. Without limiting the general application of the foregoing, the following conduct is a violation of this section:

(1) The collection of any amount (including any interest, fee, charge, or expense incidental to the principal obligation) unless such amount

is expressly authorized by the agreement creating the debt or permitted by law.

(2) The acceptance by a debt collector from any person of a check or other payment instrument postdated by more than five days unless such person is notified in writing of the debt collector's intent to deposit such check or instrument not more than ten nor less than three business days prior to such deposit.

(3) The solicitation by a debt collector of any postdated check or other postdated payment instrument for the purpose of threatening or instituting criminal prosecution.

(4) Depositing or threatening to deposit any postdated check or other postdated payment instrument prior to the date on such check or instrument.

(5) Causing charges to be made to any person for communications by concealment of the true purpose of the communication. Such charges include, but are not limited to, collect telephone calls and telegram fees.

(6) Taking or threatening to take any nonjudicial action to effect dispossession or disablement of property if:

(A) there is no present right to possession of the property claimed as collateral through an enforceable security interest;

(B) there is no present intention to take possession of the property; or

(C) the property is exempt by law from such dispossession or disablement.

(7) Communicating with a consumer regarding a debt by postcard.

(8) Using any language or symbol, other than the debt collector's address, on any envelope when communicating with a consumer by use of the mails or by telegram, except that a debt collector may use his business name if such name does not indicate that he is in the debt collection business.

SECTION 1692G. VALIDATION OF DEBTS.

(a) Notice of debt; contents.

Within five days after the initial communication with a consumer in connection with the collection of any debt, a debt collector shall, unless the following information is contained in the initial communication or the consumer has paid the debt, send the consumer a written notice containing:

(1) the amount of the debt;

(2) the name of the creditor to whom the debt is owed;

(3) a statement that unless the consumer, within thirty days after receipt of the notice, disputes the validity of the debt, or any portion thereof, the debt will be assumed to be valid by the debt collector;

(4) a statement that if the consumer notifies the debt collector in writing within the thirty-day period that the debt, or any portion thereof, is disputed, the debt collector will obtain verification of the debt or a copy of a judgment against the consumer and a copy of such verification or judgment will be mailed to the consumer by the debt collector; and

(5) a statement that, upon the consumer's written request within the thirty-day period, the debt collector will provide the consumer with the name and address of the original creditor, if different from the current creditor.

(b) Disputed debts.

If the consumer notifies the debt collector in writing within the thirty-day period described in subsection (a) that the debt, or any portion thereof, is disputed, or that the consumer requests the name and address of the original creditor, the debt collector shall cease collection of the debt, or any disputed portion thereof, until the debt collector obtains verification of the debt or a copy of a judgment, or the name and address of the original creditor, and a copy of such verification or judgment, or name and address of the original creditor, is mailed to the consumer by the debt collector.

(c) Admission of liability.

The failure of a consumer to dispute the validity of a debt under this section may not be construed by any court as an admission of liability by the consumer.

SECTION 1692H. MULTIPLE DEBTS.

If any consumer owes multiple debts and makes any single payment to any debt collector with respect to such debts, such debt collector may not apply such payment to any debt which is disputed by the consumer and, where applicable, shall apply such payment in accordance with the consumer's directions.

SECTION 1692I. LEGAL ACTIONS BY DEBT COLLECTORS.

(a) Venue.

Any debt collector who brings any legal action on a debt against any consumer shall:

(1) in the case of an action to enforce an interest in real property securing the consumer's obligation, bring such action only in a judicial district or similar legal entity in which such real property is located; or

(2) in the case of an action not described in paragraph (1), bring such action only in the judicial district or similar legal entity:

(A) in which such consumer signed the contract sued upon; or

(B) in which such consumer resides at the commencement of the action.

(b) Authorization of actions.

Nothing in this subchapter shall be construed to authorize the bringing of legal actions by debt collectors.

SECTION 1692J. FURNISHING CERTAIN DECEPTIVE FORMS.

(a) It is unlawful to design, compile, and furnish any form knowing that such form would be used to create the false belief in a consumer that a person other than the creditor of such consumer is participating in the collection of or in an attempt to collect a debt such consumer allegedly owes such creditor, when in fact such person is not so participating.

(b) Any person who violates this section shall be liable to the same extent and in the same manner as a debt collector is liable under section 1692k of this title for failure to comply with a provision of this subchapter.

1692k. CIVIL LIABILITY.

(a) Amount of damages.

Except as otherwise provided by this section, any debt collector who fails to comply with any provision of this subchapter with respect to any person is liable to such person in an amount equal to the sum of:

(1) any actual damage sustained by such person as a result of such failure;

(2)(A) in the case of any action by an individual, such additional damages as the court may allow, but not exceeding $1,000; or

(2)(B) in the case of a class action, (i) such amount for each named plaintiff as could be recovered under subparagraph (A), and (ii) such amount as the court may allow for all other class members, without regard to a minimum individual recovery, not to exceed the lesser of $500,000 or 1 per centum of the net worth of the debt collector; and

(3) in the case of any successful action to enforce the foregoing liability, the costs of the action, together with a reasonable attorney's fee as determined by the court. On a finding by the court that an action under this section was brought in bad faith and for the purpose of harassment, the court may award to defendant attorney's fees reasonable in relation to the work expended and costs.

(b) Factors considered by court.

In determining the amount of liability in any action under subsection (a), the court shall consider, among other relevant factors:

(1) in any individual action under subsection (a)(2)(A), the frequency and persistence of noncompliance by the debt collector, the nature of such noncompliance, and the extent to which such noncompliance was intentional; or

(2) in any class action under subsection (a)(2)(B), the frequency and persistence of noncompliance by the debt collector, the nature of such noncompliance, the resources of the debt collector, the number of persons adversely affected, and the extent to which the debt collector's noncompliance was intentional.

(c) Intent.

A debt collector may not be held liable in any action brought under this title if the debt collector shows by a preponderance of evidence that the violation was not intentional and resulted from a bona fide error the maintenance of procedures reasonably adapted to avoid any such error.

(d) Jurisdiction.

An action to enforce any liability created by this subchapter may be brought in any appropriate United States district court without regard to the amount in controversy, or in any other court of competent jurisdiction, within one year from the date on which the violation occurs.

(e) Advisory opinions of Commission.

No provision of this section imposing any liability shall apply to any act done or omitted in good faith in conformity with any advisory opinion of the Commission, notwithstanding that after such act or omission has occurred, such opinion is amended, rescinded, or determined by judicial or other authority to be invalid for any reason.

SECTION 1692L. ADMINISTRATIVE ENFORCEMENT.

(a) Federal Trade Commission.

Compliance with this subchapter shall be enforced by the Commission, except to the extent that enforcement of the requirements imposed under this title is specifically committed to another agency under subsection (b) of this section. For purpose of the exercise by the Commission of its functions and powers under the Federal Trade Commission Act [15 U.S.C. 41 et seq.], a violation of this subchapter shall be deemed an unfair or deceptive act or practice in violation of that Act. All of the functions and powers of the Commission under the Federal Trade Commission Act are available to the Commission to enforce compliance by any person with this subchapter, irrespective of whether that person is engaged in commerce or meets any other jurisdictional tests in the Federal Trade Commission Act, including the power to enforce the provisions of this subchapter in the same manner as if the violation had been a violation of a Federal Trade Commission trade regulation rule.

(b) Applicable provisions of law.

Compliance with any requirements imposed under this subchapter shall be enforced under:

(1) section 8 of the Federal Deposit Insurance Act [12 U.S.C. 1818], in the case of:

(A) national banks, and Federal branches and Federal agencies of foreign banks, by the Office of the Comptroller of the Currency;

(B) member banks of the Federal Reserve System (other than national banks), branches and agencies of foreign banks (other than Federal branches, Federal agencies, and insured State branches of foreign banks), commercial lending companies owned or controlled by foreign banks, and organizations operating under section 25 or 25(a) of the Federal Reserve Act [12 U.S.C. 601 et seq., 611 et seq.], by the Board of Governors of the Federal Reserve System; and

(C) banks insured by the Federal Deposit Insurance Corporation (other than members of the Federal Reserve System) and insured State branches of foreign banks, by the Board of Directors of the Federal Deposit Insurance Corporation;

(2) section 8 of the Federal Deposit Insurance Act [12 U.S.C. 1818], by the Director of the Office of Thrift Supervision, in the case of a savings association the deposits of which are insured by the Federal Deposit Insurance Corporation;

(3) the Federal Credit Union Act [12 U.S.C. 1751 et seq.] by the National Credit Union Administration Board with respect to any Federal credit union;

(4) subtitle IV of title 49, by the Secretary of Transportation, with respect to all carriers subject to the jurisdiction of the Surface Transportation Board;

(5) part A of Subtitle VII of title 49, by the Secretary of Transportation with respect to any air carrier or any foreign air carrier subject to that part; and

(6) the Packers and Stockyards Act, 1921 [7 U.S.C. 181 et Seq.], (except as provided in section 406 of that Act [7 U.S.C. 226, 227]), by the Secretary of Agriculture with respect to any activities subject to that Act.

The terms used in paragraph (1) that are not defined in this subchapter or otherwise defined in section 3(s) of the Federal Deposit Insurance Act (12 U.S.C. 1813 (s)) shall have the meaning given to them in section 1(b) of the International Banking Act of 1978 (12 U.S.C. 3101).

(c) Agency powers.

For the purpose of the exercise by any agency referred to in subsection (b) of its powers under any Act referred to in that subsection, a violation of any requirement imposed under this subchapter shall be deemed to be a violation of a requirement imposed under that Act. In addition to its powers under any provision of law specifically referred to in subsection (b), each of the agencies referred to in that subsection may exercise, for the purpose of enforcing compliance with any requirement imposed under this subchapter any other authority conferred on it by law, except as provided in subsection (d) of this section.

(d) Rules and regulations.

Neither the Commission nor any other agency referred to in subsection (b) may promulgate trade regulation rules or other regulations with respect to the collection of debts by debt collectors as defined in this subchapter.

SECTION 1692M. REPORTS TO CONGRESS BY THE COMMISSION; VIEWS OF OTHER FEDERAL AGENCIES.

(a) Not later than one year after the effective date of this subchapter and at one-year intervals thereafter, the Commission shall make reports to the Congress concerning the administration of its functions under this subchapter, including such recommendations as the Commission deems necessary or appropriate. In addition, each report of the Commission shall include its assessment of the extent to which compliance with this subchapter is being achieved and a summary of the enforcement actions taken by the Commission under section 1692l of this title.

(b) In the exercise of its functions under this subchapter, the Commission may obtain upon request the views of any other Federal agency which exercises enforcement functions under section 1692l of this title.

SECTION 1692N. RELATION TO STATE LAWS.

This subchapter does not annul, alter, or affect, or exempt any person subject to the

provisions of this subchapter from complying with the laws of any State with respect to debt collection practices, except to the extent that those laws are inconsistent with any provision of this subchapter, and then only to the extent of the inconsistency. For purposes of this section, a State law is not inconsistent with this subchapter if the protection such law affords any consumer is greater than the protection provided by this subchapter.

SECTION 1692O. EXEMPTION FOR STATE REGULATION.

The Commission shall by regulation exempt from the requirements of this subchapter any class of debt collection practices within any State if the Commission determines that under the law of that State that class of debt collection practices is subject to requirements substantially similar to those imposed by this subchapter, and that there is adequate provision for enforcement.

GLOSSARY

Acceptance—Acceptance refers to one's consent to the terms of an offer, which consent creates a contract.

Accord and Satisfaction—Accord and satisfaction refers to the payment of money, or other thing of value, which is usually less than the amount owed or demanded, in exchange for extinguishment of the debt.

Accrue—Generally, to occur or come into existence.

Accrued Interest—Interest owing but not yet paid.

Additional Principal Payment—Additional money included with a loan payment to pay off the amount owed faster thus reducing the amount of interest paid.

Amortization—The process of extinguishing or reducing a debt by periodic payments sufficient to cover current interest and part of the principal.

Annual Fee—A fee charged by a bank annually for use of a credit card.

Annual Percentage Rate (APR)—The cost of credit expressed as a yearly rate.

Anonymizer—A service that prevents Web sites from seeing a user's Internet Protocol (IP) address. The service operates as an intermediary to protect the user's identity.

Arrears—Payments which are due but not yet paid.

Asset—The entirety of a person's property, either real or personal.

Assignee—An assignee is a person to whom an assignment is made, also known as a grantee.

Assignment—An assignment is the transfer of an interest in a right or property from one party to another.

Authorized User—Any person to whom the credit card holder gives permission to use a credit card account.

Automated Teller Machines (ATMs)—Electronic terminals located on bank premises or elsewhere, through which customers of financial institutions may make deposits, withdrawals, or other transactions as they would through a bank teller.

Average Daily Balance—The method by which most credit cards calculate the credit card holder's payment, computed by adding each day's balance and dividing the total by the number of days in a billing cycle.

Bad Faith—A willful failure to comply with one's statutory or contractual obligations.

Bankrupt—The state or condition of one who is unable to pay his debts as they are, or become, due.

Bankruptcy—The legal process governed by federal law designed to assist the debtor in a new financial start while insuring fairness among creditors.

Bankruptcy Code—Refers to the Bankruptcy Act of 1978, the federal law which governs bankruptcy actions.

Bankruptcy Court—The forum in which most bankruptcy proceedings are conducted.

Bankruptcy Trustee—The person, appointed by the bankruptcy judge or selected by the creditors, who takes legal title to the property of the debtor and holds it "in trust" for equitable distribution among the creditors.

Billing Error—Any mistake in your monthly statement as defined by the Fair Credit Billing Act.

Billing Period—The number of days used to calculate interest on a loan or credit card.

Billing Statement—The monthly bill sent by a credit card issuer to the customer.

Boilerplate—Refers to standard language found almost universally in certain documents.

Breach of Contract—The failure, without any legal excuse, to perform any promise which forms the whole or the part of a contract.

Browser—A browser is special software that allows the user to navigate several areas of the Internet and view a website.

Business Days—Days counted as business days under the Truth in Lending and Electronic Fund Transfer Acts.

Capacity—Capacity is the legal qualification concerning the ability of one to understand the nature and effects of one's acts.

Caveat Emptor—Latin for "let the buyer beware."

Charge-Off—A debt deemed uncollectible by the creditor and reported as a bad debt to a credit reporting agency.

Closed-End credit—Credit that requires the borrower to repay the loaned amount without the ability to borrow any of the amount repaid.

Collateral—Property which is pledged as additional security for a debt, such as a loan.

Confession of Judgment—An admission of a debt by the debtor which may be entered as a judgment without the necessity of a formal legal proceeding.

Consideration—Something of value exchanged between parties to a contract, which is a requirement of a valid contract.

Consumer—A buyer of any consumer product.

Consumer Bankruptcy—A bankruptcy case filed to reduce or eliminate debts that are primarily consumer debts.

Consumer Credit—Credit extended to individuals to finance the purchase of goods and services arising out of consumer needs and desires.

Consumer Credit Counseling Service—A service that offers counseling to consumers and serves as a intermediary with creditors regarding debt repayment and budget planning.

Consumer Debts—Debts incurred for personal needs.

Contract—A contract is an agreement between two or more persons which creates an obligation to do or not to do a particular thing.

Cookie—When the user visits a site, a notation may be fed to a file known as a "cookie" in their computer for future reference. If the user revisits the site, the "cookie" file allows the web site to identify the user as a "return" guest and offers the user products tailored to their interests or tastes.

Cookie Buster—Software that is designed to block the placement of cookies by ad networks and Web sites thus preventing companies from tracking a user's activity.

Cosigner—Another person who signs your loan and assumes equal responsibility for it.

Credit—An advance of cash, merchandise, service, or something of value in the present in return for a promise to pay for it at some future date, usually with an agreed interest.

Credit Bureau—An agency that keeps your credit record; also called a credit-reporting agency.

Credit Card—Any card, plate, or coupon book used periodically or repeatedly to borrow money or buy goods or services on credit.

Credit History—A record of an individual's debt payments.

Credit Insurance—An insurance policy that pays off credit card debt if the borrower loses his or her job, becomes disabled, or dies.

Credit Limit—The maximum amount of charges a cardholder may apply to the account.

Credit Line—The maximum amount of money available in an open-end credit arrangement such as a credit card.

Creditor—One who is owed money.

Credit Rating—A judgment of an individual consumer's ability to repay their debts, based on current and projected income and history of payment of past debts.

Credit Report—A credit report refers to the document from a credit reporting agency setting forth a credit rating and pertinent financial data concerning a person or a company, which is used in evaluating the applicant's financial stability.

Credit Reporting Agency—A company that issues credit reports on how individual consumers manage their debts and make payments.

Credit Score—A number assigned to an individual's credit rating.

Credit Scoring System—A statistical system used to rate credit applicants according to various characteristics relevant to creditworthiness.

Credit Union—A cooperative association whose members pool their savings by purchasing shares.

Creditworthiness—Past, present and future ability to repay debts.

Criminal Impersonation—As it pertains to identity theft, means to knowingly assume a false or fictitious identity or capacity, and in that identity or capacity, doing any act with intent to unlawfully gain a benefit or injure or defraud another.

Cyberspace—Cyberspace is another name for the Internet.

Data Spill—The result of a poorly designed form on a Web site which may cause an information leak to Web servers of other companies, such as an ad network or advertising agency.

Debit Card—A plastic card, looks similar to a credit card, that consumers may use at an ATM or to make purchases, withdrawals, or other types of electronic fund transfers.

Debt—Money one person owes another.

Debt Consolidation Loan—The replacement of two or more loans with a single loan, usually with a lower monthly payment and a longer repayment period.

Debt Collector—Any person or business that regularly collects debts that are owed, or which were originally owed, to another person.

Default—The condition that occurs when a consumer fails to fulfill the obligations set out in a loan.

Delinquent—Refers to a debt that has not been paid by the payment date or by the end of any grace period.

Digital Signature—A digital signature is a digital certification or stamp that uses encryption technology to authenticate an individual's signature is legitimate.

Disclosures—Information that must be given to consumers about their financial dealings.

Download—A download is the transfer of files or software from a remote computer to the user's computer.

Electronic Fund Transfer (EFT) Systems—A variety of systems and technologies for transferring funds electronically rather than by check.

Encryption Software—Often used as a security measure, encryption software scrambles data so that it is unreadable to interceptors without the appropriate information to read the data.

Equal Credit Opportunity Act—A federal law which prohibits a creditor from discriminating against an applicant on the basis of race, religion, national origin, age, sex or marital status.

Fair Credit Billing Act—A federal law passed by Congress in 1975 to help customers resolve billing disputes with card issuers.

Fair Credit Reporting Act—A federal law that governs what credit bureaus can report concerning an individual consumer.

Fair Debt Collection Practices Act—A federal law that governs debt collection and the procedures a debt collector is permitted to follow in collecting a debt.

Federal Trade Commission—The Federal Trade Commission is an agency of the federal government created in 1914 for the purpose of promoting free and fair competition in interstate commerce.

Filter—Filter is software the user can buy that lets the user block access to websites and content that they may find unsuitable.

Finance Charge—A finance charge is any charge assessed for an extension of credit, including interest.

Financial Information—Refers to information identifiable to an individual that concerns the amount and conditions of an individual's assets, liabilities, or credit, including (a) Account numbers and balances; (b) Transactional information concerning an account; and (c) Codes, passwords, social security numbers, tax identification numbers, driver's license or permit numbers, state identification numbers and other information held for the purpose of account access or transaction initiation.

Financial Information Repository—Refers to a person engaged in the business of providing services to customers who have a credit, deposit, trust, stock, or other financial account or relationship with the person.

Firewall—A hardware or software device that controls access to computers on a Local Area Network (LAN). It examines all traffic routed between the two networks – inbound and outbound – to see if it meets certain criteria. If it does it is routed between the networks, otherwise it is stopped. It can also manage public access to private networked resources such as host applications.

Fixed Income—Income which is unchangeable.

Forbearance—A postponement of loan payments, granted by a lender or creditor, for a temporary period of time.

Fraud—A false representation of a matter of fact, whether by words or by conduct, by false or misleading allegations, or by concealment of that which should have been disclosed, which deceives and is intended to deceive another, and thereby causes injury to that person.

Garnish—To attach the wages or property of an individual.

Garnishee—A person who receives notice to hold the assets of another, which are in his or her possession, until such time as a court orders the disposition of the property.

Grace Period—The interest-free period between the transaction date and the billing date allowed by the credit card issuer provided the credit card holder does not carry a balance on their credit card.

Guarantor—One who makes a guaranty.

Guaranty—An agreement to perform in the place of another if that person reneges on a promise contained in an underlying agreement.

Home Equity Credit Line—A type of revolving credit where the borrower can borrow funds up to an established limit and the funds are secured by the borrower's home.

Installment Contract—An installment contract is one in which the obligation, such as the payment of money, is divided into a series of successive performances over a period of time.

Interest—An amount of money paid by a borrower to a lender for the use of the lender's money.

Interest Rate—The percentage of a sum of money charged for its use.

Internet—The Internet is the universal network that allows computers to talk to other computers in words, text, graphics, and sound, anywhere in the world.

Introductory Rate—The low rate charged by a lender for an initial period after which the rate increases to the indexed rate or the stated interest rate.

ISP—Refers to "Internet Service Provider"—a service that allows the user to connect to the Internet.

Joint Account—A credit account held by two or more people so that all can use the account and all assume legal responsibility to repay.

Judgment—A judgment is a final determination by a court of law concerning the rights of the parties to a lawsuit.

Judgment Creditor—A creditor who has obtained a judgment against a debtor, which judgment may be enforced to obtain payment of the amount due.

Judgment Debtor—An individual who owes a sum of money, and against whom a judgment has been awarded for that debt.

Judgment Proof—Refers to the status of an individual who does not have the financial resources or assets necessary to satisfy a judgment.

Junk E-mail—Junk e-mail is unsolicited commercial e-mail also known as "spam."

Keyword—A keyword is a word the user enters into a search engine to begin the search for specific information or websites.

Late Fee—A fee charged by a creditor when a payment does not post by the specified due date.

Late Payment—A payment made later than agreed upon in a credit contract and on which additional charges may be imposed.

Legal Capacity—Referring to the legal capacity to sue, it is the requirement that a person bringing the lawsuit have a sound mind, be of lawful age, and be under no restraint or legal disability.

Liability—Liability refers to one's obligation to do or refrain from doing something, such as the payment of a debt.

Liability On Account—Legal responsibility to repay debt.

Lien—A legal claim held by a creditor against an asset to guarantee repayment of a debt.

Links—Links are highlighted words on a website that allow the user to connect to other parts of the same website or to other websites.

Loan Principal—The loan principal is the amount of the debt not including interest or any other additions.

Material Breach—A material breach refers to a substantial breach of contract which excuses further performance by the innocent party and gives rise to an action for breach of contract by the injured party.

Maturity Date—The date upon which a creditor is designated to receive payment of a debt, such as payment of the principal value of a bond to a bondholder by the issuing company or governmental entity.

Minimum Payment—The minimum amount a credit card holder can pay to keep the account from going into default.

Minor—A person who has not yet reached the age of legal competence, which is designated as 18 in most states.

Modem—a modem is an internal or external device that connects the computer to a phone line and, if the user wishes, to a company that can link the user to the Internet.

Monthly Periodic Rate—The interest rate factor used to calculate the interest charges on a monthly basis, i.e., the yearly rate divided by 12.

Mutual Agreement—Mutual agreement refers to the meeting of the minds of the parties to a contract concerning the subject matter of the contract.

Net Income—Gross income less deductions and exemptions proscribed by law.

Net Worth—The difference between one's assets and liabilities.

Note—A writing which promises payment of a debt.

Novation—A novation refers to the substitution of a new party and the discharge of an original party to a contract, with the assent of all parties.

Obligee—An obligee is one who is entitled to receive a sum of money or performance from the obligor.

Obligor—An obligor is one who promises to perform or pay a sum of money under a contract.

Offeree—An offeree is the person to whom an offer is made.

Offeror—An offeror is the person who makes an offer.

Online Service—An online service is an ISP with added information, entertainment and shopping features.

Open-End Credit—A line of credit that may be used repeatedly, including credit cards, overdraft credit accounts, and home equity lines.

Opt-In—Refers to when a user gives explicit permission for a company to use personal information for marketing purposes.

Opt-Out—Refers to when a user prohibits a company from using personal information for marketing purposes.

Oral Agreement—An oral agreement is one which is not in writing or not signed by the parties.

Overdraft Privilege—Service offered by bank allowing customers to borrow more than the amount on deposit in their bank account.

Overlimit Fee—A fee charged by a creditor to the consumer for a balance exceeding the consumer's credit limit.

Password—A password is a personal code that the user selects to access their account with their ISP.

Past Due Fee—A fee charged by a creditor to the consumer when their account is past due.

Point of Sale (POS)—A method by which consumers can pay for purchases by having their deposit accounts debited electronically without the use of checks.

Principal—Principal is the amount of the debt not including interest or any other additions.

Privacy Policy—A privacy policy is a statement on a website describing what information about the user is collected by the site and how it is used; also known as a privacy statement or privacy notice.

Privacy Seal Program—A program that certifies a site's compliance with the standards of privacy protection. Only those sites that comply with the standards are able to note certification.

Re-Aged Account—Refers to an account status that is updated to reflect current when the account was delinquent.

Rate—Percentage a borrower pays for the use of money.

Release—A document signed by one party, releasing claims he or she may have against another party, usually as part of a settlement agreement.

Repayment Plan—A plan devised to repay debt.

Satisfaction—The discharge and release of an obligation.

Screen Name—A screen name is the name the user selects to be known by when the user communicates online.

Search Engine—A search engine is a function that lets the user search for information and websites. Search engines or search functions may be found on many web sites.

Secured Credit Card—A credit card secured by a savings deposit to ensure payment of the outstanding balance if the credit card holder defaults on payments.

Secured Loan—Borrowed money backed by collateral.

Service Charge—A component of some finance charges, such as the fee for triggering an overdraft checking account into use.

Settlement—An agreement by the parties to a dispute on a resolution of the claims, usually requiring some mutual action, such as payment of money in consideration of a release of claims.

Spam—Email from a company or charity that is unsolicited and sent to many people at one time, usually for advertising purposes; also known as junk email.

Statute of Limitations—Any law which fixes the time within which parties must take judicial action to enforce rights or thereafter be barred from enforcing them.

Stipulation—An admission or agreement made by parties to a lawsuit concerning the pending matter.

Third Party Cookie—A cookie that is placed by a party other than the user or the Web site being viewed, such as advertising or marketing groups who are trying to gather data on general consumer use third party cookies.

Truth-In-Lending Act—A federal law which requires commercial lenders to provide applicants with detailed, accurate and understandable information relating to the cost of credit, so as to permit the borrower to make an informed decision.

Unconscionable—Refers to a bargain so one-sided as to amount to an absence of meaningful choice on the part of one of the parties, together with terms which are unreasonably favorable to the other party.

Undue Influence—The exertion of improper influence upon another for the purpose of destroying that person's free will in carrying out a particular act, such as entering into a contract.

Unsecured Credit—Credit extended without collateral.

Unsecured Debt—Debt not guaranteed by the pledge of collateral, e.g. a credit card.

Unsecured Loan—An advance of money that is not secured by collateral.

URL (Uniform Resource Locator) — A URL is the address that lets the user locate a particular site. For example, http://www.ftc.gov is the URL for the Federal Trade Commission. Government URLs end in.gov and non-profit organizations and trade associations end in.org. Commercial companies generally end in.com, although additional suffixes or domains may be used as the number of Internet businesses grows.

Usurious Contract—A contract that imposes interest at a rate which exceeds the legally permissible rate.

Usury—An excessive rate of interest above the maximum permissible rate established by the state legislature.

Vendor—A seller.

Victim—As it relates to identity theft, refers to any person who has suffered financial loss or any entity that provided money, credit, goods, services or anything of value and has suffered financial loss as a direct result of the commission or attempted commission of a violation of this section.

Vitiate—To make void.

Void—Having no legal force or binding effect.

Voidable—Capable of being rendered void and unenforceable.

Website—A website is an Internet destination where the user can look at and retrieve data. All the web sites in the world, linked together, make up the World Wide Web or the "Web."

BIBLIOGRAPHY AND ADDITIONAL READING

Better Business Bureau On-Line (Date Visited: May 2007) <http://www.bbbonline.org>.

Black's Law Dictionary, Fifth Edition. St. Paul, MN: West Publishing Company, 1979.

Call For Action (Date Visited: May 2007) <http://www.callforaction.org/>.

Consumer Affairs.com (Date Visited: May 2007) <http://www.consumeraffairs.com/>.

Consumer Information Center (Date Visited: May 2007) <http://www.pueblo.gsa.gov>.

Consumer Sentinel (Date Visited: May 2007) <http://www.consumer.gov/sentinel>.

Cornell Law School Legal Information Institute. (Date Visited: May 2007) <http://www.law.cornell.edu/>.

Equifax (Date Visited: May 2007) <http://www.equifax.com/>.

Experian (Date Visited: May 2007) <http://www.experian.com/>.

Federal Deposit Insurance Corporation (Date Visited: May 2007) <http://www.fdic.gov>.

Federal Trade Commission (Date Visited: May 2007) <http://www.ftc.gov>.

National Consumer's League (Date Visited: May 2007) <http://natlconsumersleague.org>.

Nolo On-Line Encyclopedia (Date Visited: May 2007) <http://www.nolo.com>.